MINISTRY NUTS AND BOLTS

What They Don't Teach Pastors in Seminary

Aubrey Malphurs

kregel
PUBLICATIONS

Grand Rapids, MI 49501

Ministry Nuts and Bolts: What They Don't Teach Pastors in Seminary

Copyright © 1997 by Aubrey Malphurs

Published by Kregel Publications, a division of Kregel, Inc., P.O. Box 2607, Grand Rapids, MI 49501. Kregel Publications provides trusted, biblical publications for Christian growth and service. Your comments and suggestions are valued.

Scripture quotations marked GNB are from the *Good News Bible*—Old Testament: Copyright © American Bible Society 1976; New Testament: Copyright © American Bible Society 1966, 1971, 1976.

Scripture quotations marked JB are from THE JERUSALEM BIBLE, copyright © 1966 by Darton, Longman and Todd, Ltd., and Doubleday and Company, Inc. Reprinted by permission of the publisher.

Scripture quotations marked TLB are taken from The Living Bible, copyright © 1971 by Tyndale House Publishers, Wheaton, Illinois. Used by permission.

For more information about Kregel Publications, visit our web site at http:\\www.kregel.com.

Cover design: Alan G. Hartman
Book design: Nicholas G. Richardson

Library of Congress Cataloging-in-Publication Data
Malphurs, Aubrey.
    Ministry nuts and bolts: what they don't teach pastors in seminary / Aubrey Malphurs.
        p.   cm.
    Includes bibliographical references and index.
    1. Pastoral theology. 2. Clergy—Office. I. Title.
BV4011.M37   1997   253—dc21   97-41092
                                                                    CIP
ISBN 0-8254-3190-5

Printed in the United States of America

6 7 8 9 10 / 10 09 08 07 06

Contents

List of Figures and Charts

Introduction

Pastor Andrew Johnston was well into his third year at Lake Country Church, and things weren't going well. He knew that he was in trouble, and if something didn't change fairly soon, he would need to consider another ministry. The church was an average American church, consisting of seventy-five to eighty-five people, and was divided between two groups. The smaller group consisted of those people who were approximately the same age or younger than he and his wife Carolyn and who had joined after he had become pastor. The larger group was made up of those who were either a little or a lot older than he and who were members before his call to Lake Country. They had all pulled for him as their pastor, but lately they had begun to question his abilities to lead the ministry. Deep within his heart, he knew that something was wrong—perhaps they were right.

He was sitting comfortably at his dining-room table. It was 7:00 A.M. on Saturday morning, and Andy had just finished reading the morning paper. As the steam swirled upward from a freshly brewed cup of decaffeinated mocha, he began to reflect on his last three years at Lake Country Church.

Pastor Andy realized that most of his problems were in four ministry areas. First, he and the board disagreed on a significant number of ministry issues. This hadn't been true at the beginning. When he had first visited the church in view of a call, they had responded very favorably to all his ideas about the church's future ministry. He had spoken of evangelism and discipleship, and all had nodded their heads in approval. They were all for those things. What he hadn't realized was that they thought that he was going to pursue those goals himself—not get the board as well as the members to model and accomplish them. Their understanding was that they were hiring him to do the ministry; however, his understanding was that he was going to train them to do the work of the ministry.

This misunderstanding surfaced after his first anniversary at the church. The members on the board had not responded well to his attempts to meet with them privately to train them in personal evangelism. When he had brought this up in a board meeting, one of the deacons looked at him in surprise and said, "Pastor, you're the one who's been to seminary, not us. That's why we hired you! We pay you to do the work of the ministry." When Andy asked why, another board member responded, "That's the way we've always done things around here!"

By the end of his second year at Lake Country, Andy had unearthed a number of practices that he wanted to change. His approach was to ask the board and other leaders why they did what they did. They didn't appreciate all of Andy's questions—especially the *why* question. The problem was that they didn't know why. Their primary response was, "We've always done it this way." That's what they had been told when they had asked similar questions of their parents and board predecessors. But they also knew that the patent answer was no longer adequate, and it only served to frustrate Pastor Andy.

Second, the church seemed to be going nowhere. Pastor Andy hadn't noticed this when he had enlisted for his first tour of ministry duty with the church. Now the first image that popped into Andy's mind was that of a crippled ship adrift on the ocean. His church had no direction. Seminary had taught Andy to preach, and that's what he did every Sunday. The tacit assumption was that 95 percent of pastoral ministry was preaching. The other 5 percent consisted of such things as weddings, funerals, visitation, and board meetings. These were things that the average preacher learned to put up with.

After a year of preaching, the initial excitement of his coming had worn off. He noted that he wasn't getting the same response to his sermons as at the beginning of his ministry. Some members, mostly women, seemed to be listening and some occasionally took notes. But most people weren't as responsive, and some sat and fidgeted while others stared out the windows.

It was during this time that Andy first began to wrestle with his feelings of frustration over the ministry. This unleashed a series of questions that seemed to come from nowhere: Is this what church is all about? Is this what I spent three years of my life in seminary preparing to do? The thought of experiencing this for the rest of his life was frightening and depressing. As he thought further about it, other questions formed, such as: What is this church supposed to be doing? Is this what Christ called me to do? And is this what Christ called his church to do—to show up every Sunday and listen to my preaching? He concluded that there had to be more to ministry than this.

Third, not only was the church going nowhere, but the people gave little thought to the church's future. They simply assumed that it would always be there and do what it had always done. One Sunday a guest speaker had asked the people: "When you close your eyes and think about this church five years, ten years, even twenty years from now, what do you see?" Most sat and stared with puzzled expressions on their faces. No one had ever asked such a question. One of the board members brought it up at the next meeting, and most concurred that they had not thought that much about the church's future except that they needed an infusion of youth or there might not be a future. When they closed their eyes and envisioned the future, they didn't see much of anything beyond business as usual. When Pastor Andy closed his eyes and pictured the church's future, he envisioned it no differently either. That is when he had begun to question if he had made a big mistake. Maybe he wasn't cut out to be a pastor!

Fourth, the assumption in seminary was that discipleship took place primarily as the result of the communication of Scripture, whether preaching or teaching (the homileticians urged the former and the academics the latter). Pastor Andy had some exposure to the ministry of Campus Crusade during his schooling, and they had sold him on a one-on-one or small-group-driven model for discipleship, not the pulpit-driven model of seminary. He was more than a little confused. He believed that he was an above-average preacher (he had made Bs on most of his sermons), and he enjoyed preaching a good sermon—though it didn't happen every Sunday.

Like so many other pastors in the twenty-first century, he observed that people didn't faithfully show up every Sunday to hear him preach. He estimated that most attended the worship service about two or three times a month at best. Also, Andy concluded that if preaching is the key to discipleship, then mediocre wouldn't do. He needed to be good—real good, which admittedly he wasn't. But he took some solace in the fact that few of his classmates were that good either. He hoped that in spite of stumbling that first year he would get better. His seminary professor had assured his class of budding homileticians that, with experience, most of them would improve.

A careful analysis of Andy's four primary areas of struggle reveals that his preparation for pastoral ministry had neglected four foundational ministry concepts. The first foundational ministry concept is core values. Whenever people don't get along or differ over major ministry decisions in a church—whether it involves a leadership board or a Sunday school class—the problem often lies in the area of their core values. The *why* question that Andy regularly posed to the board gets at a ministry's core values. Whether he's aware of it or not, every pastor has a core-values set. The same is true for the church. And it's these organizational values that drive all that a ministry does. When a pastor and a board hold to different values, they will seldom agree on the direction of the ministry.

Certainly human nature can and does often play a major part in any disagreement. One of the acts of the sinful nature according to Galatians 5:20 is discord and dissension, but there are times when godly men disagree at a fundamental ministry level. This was true in the case of Paul and Barnabas in Acts 15:36–41. This may have been the case at Lake Country Church. Regardless, Pastor Andy's core values are significantly different from the board's, and neither is aware of what is driving those differences. It is these fundamental differences that are leading to much of the disagreement between the pastor and the board. For example, the problem over who is to do the work of the church's ministry—the pastor or the people—is as much a values problem as it is a theological issue.

The second foundational ministry concept is mission. That the church is drifting in no particular direction indicates that it doesn't have a clear, compelling, ministry direction. It might have gotten by with this in the church-friendly culture of the 1940s and 1950s but not in the skeptical culture that characterizes the 1990s and beyond. Pastor Andrew asked: What is this church supposed to be doing? The *what* question is the mission question. What does the Bible say that it should be doing? That no one could answer the mission question is a sure sign that the church is in serious trouble. It doesn't know where it's going nor what it's supposed to be doing. These are mission issues.

The third foundational ministry concept is vision. Vision as well as mission has everything to do with the church's future. It's a mental picture of what the ministry's tomorrow will look like. It's a snapshot of the church's future and all its exciting possibilities. That the board in particular and the people in general don't have a vision is not a good sign. While this church isn't entirely aware of it, it's in serious trouble. Business as usual will not suffice in the information age when change is a constant. A church that is without a clear vision of its future places that future in jeopardy. It desperately needs a preferred future. Instead, it harbors a museum mentality; it mirrors church life and leadership in a bygone era.

The fourth foundational ministry concept is strategy. Every church has a strategy. It may be a good one or a bad one. The latter is the situation at Lake Country. One reason why it is bad is that strategies exist to implement missions, and Lake Country doesn't have a mission. Another is that the present strategy is based on some past mission that long since has been lost and forgotten. A third is that the present strategy simply isn't working. That strategy mirrors an outdated three-to-thrive mentality that consists of three meetings a week: A Sunday morning service including a Sunday school, a Sunday evening service, and a Wednesday night prayer meeting.

The people's expectations for all these meetings are that the pastor will preach a sermon or at least teach a Bible lesson. Pastor Andy has been faithful to those expectations. The people, though, also "vote with their feet." While an interest in prayer exists, only a handful of faithful old-timers show up for Wednesday night prayer meeting. Also, Sunday night attendance has dropped dramatically over the past ten years to the point that Pastor Andy wonders if they should cancel the meeting. So far they continue to meet because he enjoys teaching the Bible on Sunday nights, and the board members believe that to cancel Sunday night church sends the wrong message to the people.

Of the church's three meetings, most people will attend the Sunday morning worship service. Their attendance fluctuates, on average, between two and three times a month. If people can be discipled from the pulpit alone, which is doubtful, then two or three sermons a month aren't sufficient to make disciples. Actually, most congregants at Lake Country aren't sure what a disciple is. If you asked, they would confess that they wouldn't know what a disciple looks like even if one walked through the front door of the church.

The tragedy of all this is twofold. First, Lake Country's problem goes beyond this small church. It's the problem facing a significant number of older churches all across North America—they're in deep trouble. In what has become a predominantly secular culture, small churches are becoming a thing of the past. Lyle Schaller summarizes it best when he writes that "two-thirds to three-fourths of all congregations founded before 1960 are either on a plateau in size or shrinking in number."[1]

Second, Pastor Andrew completed the typical basic training for pastors at a very fine evangelical institution. He graduated near the top of his class with the assumption that he was prepared to pastor a church. He has learned the hard way, however, that he wasn't. The idea that pastoral ministry is to be equated with the pulpit is fallacious and unbiblical. A quick survey of the epistles reveals that Paul, and others who often functioned in pastoral roles, spent as much time evangelizing the lost as they did preaching to and teaching the saved. While this assumption worked to some extent in a sympathetic, churched culture of the past, it doesn't in the unsympathetic, unchurched culture in which pastors find themselves today. As they say in the South: "That dog won't hunt." Unfortunately for seminary graduates, many of our classical evangelical seminaries appear to have missed the paradigm shift that has taken place in our culture. Instead, they are preparing pastors to minister as if we are still living back in the 1940s and 1950s.

This isn't to argue that preaching and teaching the Bible aren't important. Nothing could be further from the truth. The proclamation of God's word is central and essential to any ministry because Scripture is truth (John 17:17), and today's lost and dying generation desperately needs to hear biblical truth. Ministry, though, must not be primarily equated with the communication of biblical truth from a pulpit in a sanctuary or a podium in a classroom.

Neither is a pastor to be solely equated with a preacher. If the typical church's difficult days of the 1980s and 1990s have taught us anything, they have taught us that the pastor needs to be a leader and a coach of leaders as well as a preacher. Yet, if one peruses the catalogs of many of our best evangelical schools, he or she will discover only one or, at the most, two courses on leadership. In spite of the fact that every church survives on the basis of competent lay leadership, future pastors graduate not knowing how to recruit and train these leaders.

Preaching alone will not get the job done. To obey the Savior's command and make disciples (Matt. 28:19), the preaching and teaching of God's Word must be accompanied by a vigorous small-group ministry that helps congregants discuss, understand, and apply God's truth to their lives as well as hold them accountable for the same. It's in small groups that Christians realize community. It's in community that believers experience all the "one another" passages of the New Testament. Another quick perusal of a typical seminary catalog, however, discloses only an occasional elective in small-group ministry.

It's imperative that those who would lead and pastor the newer paradigm churches of the twenty-first century must think about vital leadership and ministry concepts such as core values, mission, vision, and strategy and how they relate to one another (see figure I.1). The reason is that these core values make up the ministry ABCs. While there are other ministry ABCs (character development, stewardship, and so forth) the core values form the fundamental nuts and bolts of any ministry. The evangelical churches that God is blessing in North America have carefully thought through these concepts and positioned themselves accordingly. Thus, it behooves the rest of the churches to learn from their examples and pursue the same if the future church is to have maximum impact for the Savior in the third millennium.

I have written this book to help leaders, pastors, and church boards think through these ministry ABCs. Part 1 consists of three chapters that will help leaders understand, discover, and develop their own core values as well as those that drive their ministries. Part 2 presents two chapters on defining and then developing a mission for ministry. Part 3 provides

Figure I.1: Leadership and Ministry Concepts

three chapters on the vision concept. The first chapter defines a ministry vision. The second chapter distinguishes the vision from a mission. The last chapter will assist leaders in developing a vision statement for their ministries. Part 4 consists of two chapters on defining and then developing a strategy that is tailor-made for each ministry.

I have included discussion questions at the end of each chapter designed to help individual leaders grasp and apply the ideas in each chapter. I recommend that pastors and board members read this book together and discuss the ideas as a group. The questions will help leaders raise as well as wrestle with the tough issues that some might otherwise avoid.

Notes

1. Randy Frazee with Lyle Schaller, *The Comeback Congregation* (Nashville: Abingdon, 1995), 11.

Part 1

The Values of Your Ministry

1

The Definition of Core Values

What Is a Credo?

As Pastor Andy walked through the front door, the clock on the living-room desk chimed 11:30 P.M. Carolyn had already gone to bed but was still wide awake. She called from their bedroom, "I thought your meeting with the board would be over by nine."

"It was another one of those meetings like the last one," said a weary Andy. "We couldn't agree on much of anything. Seems like every time we meet, we fight about something. I'm so angry with Harry Smith that I could strangle him. I'm convinced that he intentionally opposes all of my proposals simply because they're my ideas. And he's not very pleasant about the way he does it. Sometimes he gets so mad at me, that I can see the veins in his forehead and neck."

As he got ready for bed, he mused: *Perhaps this is God's way of telling us that it's time to move on to another ministry. Maybe we missed his leading when we took this church. Right now life is miserable, and I can't take much more of this.*

Why is there so much disagreement among Lake Country Church's board of leaders? As pastor, is Andy the spiritual giant and the board a group of spiritual pygmies? Did he make a mistake in accepting the pastorate of the church? Could this be God's way of simply moving him on to another ministry? While there is no guarantee that all on the board, including Pastor Andy, are walking with Christ, the answer to all of these questions most likely is an emphatic no. Many of the real problems lie at the core-values level, and the tragedy is that no one knows it. What typically happens in these situations is that the pastor hears God's call to another church or returns to the seminary to pursue doctoral studies. A distressing response from an increasing number of ministers in this type of situation is for them to drop out of ministry to pursue a nonministry profession. Meanwhile, the church hires another pastor, and unless their values coalesce, they repeat the same cycle.

So what can a church do? And what is a pastor's job as leader in these circumstances? A vital aspect of pastoral leadership today is to make sure that the ministry organization knows itself. There are certain durable core values or beliefs that underlie and define every organization—whether it's a church, a parachurch ministry, or a marketplace entity. Core values are fundamental to all that the organization does. They are ministry defining and have everything to do with a ministry's distinctiveness. They are what distinguishes one ministry from another, and they explain why some people are attracted to your church while others are repelled. They dictate personal involvement. If an individual's core values align with the ministry's, that individual is more likely to invest his or her life in that ministry. Values communicate what is important—the organization's bottom line. Thus, core values define God's heart for your ministry or church.

Values are responsible for a number of other things as well. They not only inspire people to ministry, but they also enhance your leadership as well as shape the very character of your ministry. Most often, values are key to a church's success or failure. Consequently, to say that discovering and establishing core values is important might be an understatement—they are critical to the existence of your ministry. In *Rediscovering Church*, pastor Bill Hybels writes: "In fact, establishing the core principles is so important that I'll be devoting an entire chapter to the values that Willow Creek's leaders have identified as central to accomplishing our mission."[1] Unfortunately for Andy and the church, no one has ever instructed them in the importance of the ministry basics, or in this case, the importance of identifying and understanding their essential values.

Since a ministry's core values are so important, we must pursue the question: What are core organizational values? The purpose of this chapter is to answer that question. I will begin by defining what core values aren't. Next, I will provide a foundational working definition of what they are. Finally, I'll build on that foundation by examining the various kinds of values.

What Core Values Are Not

Those who write on leadership and the organizational basics often confuse values with other key concepts. This makes it difficult for ministry leaders who desire to identify and work with these concepts. I draw a sharp line between the God-honoring values and the mission, vision, strategy, and doctrinal statements of a ministry.

Values Are Not a Mission

First, do not make the mistake of equating your set of ministry values with your ministry mission. As we will discover in part 2 of this book, your ministry mission is a statement of what your ministry is supposed to accomplish. Your core values are not the same as your mission. They answer the *why* question for your ministry. They explain why you do what you do, supplying the God-ordained reasons behind what you do. They not only shape your congregational culture but dictate the precise biblical mission that you choose for your ministry.

Values Are Not a Vision

Second, do not confuse your fundamental values with your ministry vision. Like the mission, your vision also addresses what your ministry is supposed to be doing according to the Bible. Whereas the mission states in one sentence what you plan to accomplish, the vision paints a picture of the same. The mission involves the hill your army needs to take; the vision is what your army will look like on top of the hill.

Your ministry values should differ from your vision in at least three fundamental ways. First, like your ministry mission, the vision also answers the *what* question. It provides a clear snapshot of what the church is supposed to be doing. The central values answer the *why* question, providing the reasons for your vision.

Second, contrary to what many believe, a church isn't vision driven. It is values driven and vision focused. On the one hand, when a ministry takes the time to carefully articulate its vision, its future comes into focus. The people who make up that ministry are better able to see the future; they can envision what they're supposed to be doing. On the other hand, when a ministry has a shared set of beliefs, it knows what is driving those beliefs. Values move the ministry. They are the hidden motivators that dictate every decision it makes, every problem it solves, and every dollar it spends.

Third, every ministry, whether church or parachurch, has a core set of values. The ministry may or may not be aware of those values, and the values may be good or bad. Regardless, a values set is present because something drives the ministry. A church, however, may not have a vision. One of the reasons why so many churches sprinkled across North America today are in trouble is because they have neither a vision nor a mission. They haven't given much thought to what their future looks like; consequently, their future looks grim.

Values Are Not a Strategy

Third, you will confuse those in your ministry if you equate your values with your strategy. While your primary beliefs answer the *why* question, your strategy answers the *how* question. Values dictate the mission you choose for your ministry. Values will also determine the strategy that you select to implement that mission in your ministry community. Your strategy addresses how you will realize your mission. The early church adopted Christ's Great Commission mandate (Matt. 28:19; Mark 16:15) as their mission statement (Acts 1:8). Their strategy for realizing this mission primarily consisted of the three missionary journeys that Luke recorded in Acts 13–14; 15:36–18:22; and 18:23–21:16. The biblical values that surfaced in ministries such as the church at Jerusalem (Acts 2:42–47) deeply influenced this strategy.

Values Are Not a Doctrinal Statement

Fourth, my experience has been that many leaders and lay people confuse the sound set of fundamental values with the doctrinal statement of theological beliefs. When I conduct a seminar on developing a statement of values, called a credo, people often raise their hands and ask if I'm talking about developing a doctrinal statement for their churches. My answer is an emphatic, "No!" Most have a doctrinal statement; few, if any, have a credo or statement of primary values.

The key precept that drives the ministry and dictates what its mission, vision, and strategy will be is the credo. A church's doctrinal statement is a written document of its collected theological beliefs regarding such vital concepts as God, the Bible, the Trinity, Christ, the Holy Spirit, man, sin, angels, salvation, the church, and the future state. It's possible that some slight overlap could exist with a credo, such as the importance of the Scriptures in directing the ministry or the Great Commission as the church's mission. Regardless, when you compare a church's credo with its doctrinal statement, the difference is obvious. Consequently, I've provided an example of one church's credo and its doctrinal statement in appendix A. Compare the two and you'll quickly discern the differences.

What Core Values Are

Now that we understand what core values are not, let's define what they are. I define a Christian organization's values as the constant, passionate, biblical core beliefs that drive the ministry (see figure 1.1). Core values consist of five vital components.

Core Values Are Constant

In the past, some old-timers caustically stated that the only thing you can be sure of is death and taxes. Today, we must add change. Secular writers tell us that change is now a constant, and they're right. North America is in transition from the modern to the postmodern era. Whenever any country moves from one era into another, it will always be accompanied by a white-water kind of change that affects the social, economic, political, and technological arenas of that country.

An example from the technological realm is the personal-computer revolution. No one questions the truth that the computer has affected millions of lives within a short time and that it will lead us into the next revolution—the so-called information highway. In his book *The Road Ahead*, Bill Gates writes that "the information highway will transform our culture as dramatically as Gutenberg's press did the Middle Ages."[2] Already, computers track every check we write, every phone call we make, and every transaction on our credit cards. All the world's information—whether its medical knowledge, shopping catalogs, books, and so forth—will be within the reach of potentially billions of people.

The question for the church is: How will it choose to respond to all of this accelerating change? In the 1950s and 1960s it chose to ignore it. The typical church of that period functioned at a pace that was from five to twenty years behind our culture. Consequently, many a church has been out of touch with the people as well as the technology that could help it conduct its ministry more efficiently. Some churches are convinced that the computer is a tool of the Antichrist, and they still prefer to use a mimeograph and stencil over a copier.

The key to dealing with change is determining what will help the church versus what will hurt it. But how is this possible? One way is to discover and articulate your ministry's fundamental hierarchy of values. In Acts 2:42–47, Luke reveals that the Jerusalem Church understood its values (see appendix B). This helped them navigate their ministry ship through the sea of change that was taking place all around them as they struggled to move from an era of law to an era of grace. It also helped the Twelve in Acts 6:1–7 determine and focus their ministry (prayer and the ministry of the Word) during a problematic time when they could have drifted off course.

If a ministry's core values are to guide it through difficult times of transition, those values must not be in transition. If the values drive the ministry and if they change every other year, then the ministry will constantly be changing directions. The result will be chaos because one year the church may conduct an all-out assault on one hill only to change to another hill the following year. At one moment the church targets the believing community, consisting of the already convinced. The next moment, the church has decided to change course and target unchurched lost people—the unconvinced. This leaves followers confused, bewildered, and angry.

Throughout a leaders' growth and development as well as that of his or her ministry, there will be times of transition during which values formation takes place. An example is when a leader, such as Pastor Andy, attends a university or theological seminary. Andy left seminary with some values that he didn't have when he matriculated. He also jettisoned a few. As he continues to stretch and grow as a leader, he will both adopt and drop other values. To a certain extent, Andy and most pastors constantly define and hone the unique set of values that undergird their ministries—here a tweak and there a tweak. It's imperative, however, that they reach a point in their ministry development when those beliefs don't change appreciably.

Another period of transition for the leader is a ministry-paradigm shift. The older, preboomer generation of North American pastors are facing this dilemma. They were trained under an older paradigm for ministry that was primarily pulpit driven. People also followed their leadership simply because of the authority of their positions—congregants did what the pastor asked because he was the pastor.

The newer churches in North America, while attempting to be strong in the pulpit, appear to be moving toward a small-group-driven paradigm. Much of the ministry takes place in small-group communities, and pastors find themselves spending a significant portion of their time training the leaders of these groups. There is also more emphasis on evangelism and more interest in reaching seekers and the unchurched. People no longer follow the pastor because he is the pastor. Instead, they carefully scrutinize his character and examine his vision and values. They ask: Do my vision and values align with those of the pastor? This paradigm shift is challenging a number of middle-aged pastors who face ministry in the third millennium to return to and reexamine their values.

Core Values Are Passionate

Whereas vision is a "seeing" word, passion is a "feeling" word. Leaders feel passionately about their core beliefs. Every leader has numerous values, but they are passionate about a few. Your intellect will tell you what your values are. If you conduct a values inventory, you might list fifty to one hundred values. Your heart will tell you which of those values are priority—which ones you are passionate about.

Core beliefs do more than build a fire in your heart and stir your emotions. They move you to action. You can't walk away from your core values unmoved, or they aren't core values. Core values are infectious. They leave you with a sense that you must do something about them. They move or drive you toward the vision—from what is to what ought to be. If I value authentic biblical community, then you will find me in some sort of small group. If I value prayer, then you'll frequently find me on my knees. If lost people matter to me, then I'll spend time with them. If evangelism is at the core, then I'll become a contagious Christian.

The early church not only valued prayer (Acts 2:42), they were passionate about prayer. Consequently, hardly a biblical scene slips by when they aren't spending time in prayer (Acts 1:14; 6:4, 6; 8:15; 12:5, 12; 13:3; 14:23; 20:36). They were also passionate about people. They healed sick people (Acts 3:6–10) and witnessed to lost people (Acts 10). They even went so far as to put needy people before material possessions (Acts 2:45; 4:32).

Core Values Are Biblical

The core values that make up a ministry's credo should be Bible based. If you look through the credos in appendix B, you will note that several actually provide biblical references. Saddleback Valley Community Church of Mission Viejo, California, lists seventeen core values. Every value has at least one passage of Scripture, some have two or three, and one has five. Other churches may not quote or reference a passage of Scripture but the values are obviously Bible based. Willow Creek Community Church of Barrington, Illinois, states: "We believe that lost people matter to God, and, therefore, ought to matter to us." Though they provide no biblical text, such passages as Luke 15 and Luke 19:1–10 prove the point.

Some values don't appear to have Scriptural warrant. You read them and wonder what the biblical basis might be. For example, Lakeview Community Church values creativity and innovation. They state the following:

> An Appreciation for Creativity and Innovation—In today's rapidly changing world, forms and methods must be continually evaluated, and if necessary, altered to fit new conditions. While proven techniques should not be discarded at whim, we encourage creativity and innovation, flexibility and adaptability. We are more concerned with effectiveness in ministry than with adherence to tradition.[3]

A student once challenged: "Where might you find creativity and innovation in the Scriptures?" My response was: "That's easy, try Genesis 1." Again, Willow Creek Community Church states: "We believe that life-change happens best in small groups."[4] Some would question where small groups are found in the Bible. The answer is in Acts 2:46–47; 5:4; 12:12, and other passages in the epistles. Their contexts document that life change characterized those who were a part of these early biblical communities. For example, Acts 2:46–47 states that the early church ate together with glad and sincere hearts while giving praise to God. In my experience so far, I've been able to find a biblical reference for the core values found in most credos.

But must every value in a credo be biblically based? There is a significant difference in the words *should be* and *must be*. On the one hand, I prefer that there be a biblical text for every belief. The true test of a central value is: Is it scriptural? If there is no biblical basis, then perhaps it's not biblical. On the other hand, I believe that all truth is God's truth. And while all the content of the Bible is true (John 17:17), not all truth is found in the Bible. It is true that one plus one equals two, yet I don't find that in my Bible. The problem is: How can we know if something is true when it's not found in the Bible? Scientific evidence is not always reliable. The best scientific minds once believed that the earth, not the sun, was the center of the solar system. I believe that it's possible to have values based on God's truth that aren't found in the Scriptures. These are more characteristic of for-profit marketplace organizations such as health facilities, retail stores, grocery stores, and restaurants than of decidedly Christian ministries that are nonprofit organizations.

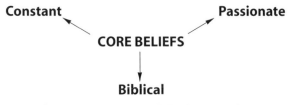

Figure 1.1: Vital Values-Defining Components

Core Values Are Core Beliefs

Two characteristics of core values are that they are core beliefs. First, they are core. If you were to list all your organizational values, the list would be long, depending on the time you took to perform this task. The more time you took, the longer the list. I have looked through the values found in the sample credos in my book *Values-Driven Leadership* and discovered that there are around one hundred, though some are worded differently. These are all important because they affect your ministry organization in some way. Some, however, influence your church more than do others. If you returned to your list of values, most likely you would find the more important values first in the list with the least important values toward the end. Your most important beliefs are your core values. They are essential to what you do. They dictate what you believe is God's heart for your ministry and are found at the top of your priority list.

Second, your core values are your beliefs. As I said earlier in this chapter, core values aren't the kinds of beliefs that are found in a doctrinal statement. They are not representative of the church's theological beliefs, though they are based on theology. The deity of the Holy Spirit and one's view of the end times are central to the theology of any church, but these truths probably won't drive the church.

Some synonyms for your values or beliefs are: *convictions*, *precepts*, *ideals*, *standards*, and *assumptions*. Values or beliefs are the organization's fundamental set of convictions on which it premises all of its actions and policies. They are the deep, intrinsic precepts that define your ministry organization. They mirror the essence of your ministry and what you will accomplish as the result of holding to them. If you examine them carefully, you'll see that they are the primary hidden motivators of your entire church or parachurch ministry. If you review the values of the Jerusalem Church either in Acts 2:42–47 or appendix B against the backdrop of the entire book of Acts, you will quickly discover that they define the very heart of the church. They explain why the church accomplished what it accomplished in the book of Acts and beyond.

Core Values Drive Your Ministry

Your church's primary beliefs move the ministry in a particular, unique direction. Earlier in this chapter, I stated that every ministry is vision focused and values driven. Values sit in the driver's seat of your ministry vehicle. They quietly (but sometimes not so quietly) drive the ministry in a particular direction. I call this the "values effect" (see chart 1.1 for a summary). An understanding of your core precepts explains your ministry's behavior and why it behaves the way that it does. They affect everything that you do. This section, however, will focus on six vital ministry areas: decision making, problem solving, risk taking, goal setting, team building, and financial spending.

Decision Making. Your fundamental precepts direct every decision that you make. Perhaps this sounds mundane; however, you must realize that each day you potentially make hundreds of decisions that affect your ministry, depending on the size of your church or parachurch ministry. Although the majority of the decisions are minor, they add up over time.

Some decisions require a yes or a no in response. Others call for a choice between that which is good and that which is better, as Paul mentions in Philippians 1:9–10. Regardless, the question is: How can you and your team know what is the best decision in your ministry context? First, consider the fact that you may not be able to make the best decision. This is true largely for the ministry that hasn't taken the time to discover and articulate its core beliefs. Leaders' values are directing their decisions—only each unknowingly holds to a different set of values and finds himself or herself regularly locked in conflict over the decisions to be made. This is the situation at Lake Country Church. The board essentially holds one common core-values set while Pastor Andy holds another. Their distinctive values sets are driving their decisions in different directions, and they regularly find themselves locked in conflict. If they are able to reach a decision, it's often the result of compromise, not consensus, and most are unhappy with the outcome.

Second, realize that you can make a much better decision when you know and understand that your key shared values are directing your decisions. This motivates you and your ministry team to discover those values and articulate a credo so that all are consciously aware of why they believe the way they do. Then the seemingly minor decisions will be made intuitively from a similar or common values pool. You'll make the so-called major decisions based on your stated credo. The point person on the team will present the choice that has to be made and then articulate the value or values that he or she believes will influence or direct the final decision.

In Acts 6:1–7 the Twelve faced a difficult dilemma. The widows of the Grecian Jews were being overlooked in the daily administration of food. The Twelve had a decision to make. Would they add to their job descriptions by personally taking care of this responsibility? At the top of their leadership priorities was prayer and the ministry of the Word (compare Acts 6:2, 4 with Acts 2:42). But they also valued people—in this case—widows. Their decision though emotionally painful was intellectually simple. To add another responsibility to their job descriptions would cause them to neglect their primary values—prayer and the ministry of the Word. So they chose to assign the care of the widows to other capable people.

Problem Solving. Your core values dictate how you resolve your problems. There are three steps that lead to effective problem solving. First, all those directly involved in the decision should meet together and determine the exact nature of the problem. Then they should conduct a problem analysis. This involves collecting all the data or information necessary to solve the problem. They should ask: What are the facts? How have others facing similar problems solved them? Finally, the team should determine what the viable solutions are and then select the best solution.

It is in the last step that values exert the most influence. The problem solvers must ask: How do our core biblical values address the problem? What solution do our primary beliefs dictate? If we've already made a decision, does it complement or contradict our values?

A case in point is the early church in Acts. The problem was: How do we take care of our poor and those in need among us? The church at Jerusalem felt an obligation to address not only the spiritual needs but also the physical needs of its people, both intricately entwined. What should they do? Clearly they valued their people above their material possessions. On the basis of this value, they chose to hold everything they owned in common and sell their material possessions to share with and take care of those in need (Acts 2:44–45; 4:32).

Risk Taking. My observation of today's Christian leaders who are having a powerful impact for God, such as Rick Warren and Tony Evans, is that they are risk takers. This was also true in the first century. Acts 15:24 describes Barnabas and Paul as "men who have risked their lives for the name of our Lord Jesus Christ." While few seem to delight in taking risks, every ministry must take some if it hopes to make a difference for Christ. Risk taking walks hand in hand with effective ministry.

The problem with taking risks is the fear of failure. No one likes to fail. We all want to be winners. Risk taking by its very nature makes leaders vulnerable to failure. One way to address this problem is to value people to the point that you allow them to be human and make mistakes. Thus, you create a ministry environment where people are free to be creative and innovative. An example from the marketplace is 3COM, an employer who tells its employees that if they aren't making at least ten mistakes a day, then they're not trying hard enough. Creative, innovative ministries are risky ventures. But they characterize churches that are making a God-honoring difference in our post-Christian culture.

Goal Setting. Your fundamental beliefs determine the goals that you set for your ministry. Your goals are accurate reflections of your values. The high-impact church that will make a powerful difference in the twenty-first century is goal-oriented. Your organizational values will determine which goals you set and which goals you reject. If one of your values is evangelism, then one of your goals will be reaching lost people. If another value is worship or teaching, then your goals reflect both of these elements in some way.

Team Building. New Testament ministry is team ministry. This is because ministry always takes place best in the context of a team of multigifted and multitalented people. Christ conducted his three-and-a-half-year ministry with a team of struggling disciples. Paul always surrounded himself with a ministry team. One of the most discouraging portions of the New Testament is found in 2 Timothy 4:9–18 where Paul is in prison and all alone.

The ministry team, however, must be able to work together. Pastor Andy and his board make up a team that you would find in a typical small church all across North America. They found it difficult, if not impossible, to work together. The potential solution to these and other similar team problems is the discovery and articulation of the organization's core values. The organization must hold more values in common than not. Otherwise, they can be certain of constant conflict until there is a change of heart or a division.

Financial Spending. Finally, your core values will dictate every dollar you spend in the ministry. Statements about finances tend to grab the attention of most pastors, board members, and treasurers. The truth is that it takes finances to conduct any ministry whether it be a church or parachurch organization. A recent study reveals that monetary giving in churches over the last twenty years is at an all-time low. There are numerous reasons for this. One obvious reason is the televangelist scandals of the 1980s. People want to hang on to their money, and these scandals have given many a lasting excuse not to part with it. Another is the poor spiritual condition of so many churches today. Most people know a poor investment when they see one, and they ask themselves: Why pour my money into a ministry that is accomplishing so little for the Savior and that may be in the early stages of rigor mortis?

Regardless of why people aren't giving, the church must spend its money wisely. It will spend money on that which it values—whether right or wrong, and it refuses to spend money on what it doesn't value. A church may say that it values evangelism and desires to reach lost people, but one cursory glance at the budget might reveal otherwise. In fact, a ministry's budget will tell you everything about its values. In the midst talking about money, the Savior says in Matthew 6:21: "For where your treasure is, there your heart will be also." You can tell from the budget how much a church values its pastor, children, evangelism, facilities, worship, and so on. Often, you can prioritize the ministry values according to the money assigned to each program.

THE VALUES EFFECT
Decision Making
Problem Solving
Risk Taking
Goal Setting
Team Building
Finances Spent

Chart 1.1: The Values Effect

Kinds of Values

To gain a clear understanding of core values, we have looked at what they aren't and then defined what they are. We can accrue additional understanding by examining the different kinds and characteristics of values.

Conscious Versus Unconscious Values

The key fundamental beliefs of a Christian ministry exist at a conscious or unconscious level. As I conduct seminars and consult with ministry organizations, I find that most hold their values at an unconscious level. That's one reason why I often refer to them as hidden motivators. Like Pastor Andy and the board at Lake Country Church, people have ministry-defining precepts but aren't completely aware of what they are nor the impact that they exert on their ministries.

Consequently, it becomes the leaders' responsibility to discover and communicate the values of their churches. By moving them from the unconscious to the conscious level, all will essentially know why they are doing what they are doing. If they hold to certain unbiblical standards, they will know what they are and have the opportunity to change them. If they find themselves in constant disagreement, they'll know precisely where the problems lie.

The Jerusalem Church seems to have been conscious of its fundamental values. Otherwise, Luke might not have been able to articulate them as he did in Acts 2:42–47. In Acts 2:42 he says that "they devoted themselves to" their values. They knew them at a conscious level because they lived them at a conscious level.

Shared Versus Unshared Values

Common cause is essential to accomplishing all that Christ has called us to do. Common cause starts with shared values. Without question, the reason that the early church was so effective is because of its shared values. If Pastor Andy and his board were to identify the beliefs that are driving their decisions, they would find that most are not shared. Had they known this before the church's marriage to Andy as its pastor, it would have saved all of them much grief. If a ministry board is to work together, it must share to a great degree its basic values.

Kouzes and Posner conducted research that involved over 2,300 managers at varying levels and discovered that shared values

- foster strong feelings of personal effectiveness,
- promote high levels of company loyalty,
- facilitate consensus about key organization goals and stakeholders,
- encourage ethical behavior,

- promote strong norms about working hard and caring,
- reduce levels of job stress and tension.[5]

While it is doubtful that Kouzes and Posner included any Christian ministries in their survey, certainly church and parachurch ministries could benefit from these same results.

Many American churches at the dawn of the twenty-first century find themselves in a struggle for survival. A common characteristic of this struggle for survival is sagging attendance. One solution that a number of churches have pursued is to merge—by joining forces their chances of survival are much better. On the surface this seems to make good sense; however, I know of few mergers that have worked. Most often they either split or one of the merged parties eventually disperses to other churches. While there are numerous reasons why mergers tend to fail, a primary factor is unshared values.

Christians who hold to common precepts feel empowered to accomplish a mission; are intensely loyal to a cause; feel a deeper sense of effectiveness; work harder; and most importantly, they care deeply about one another and want to minister together. According to Acts 4:32, Luke writes that the Jerusalem Church had achieved common cause: "All the believers were one in heart and mind." Acts 2:42–47 would seem to indicate that a major cause for this was shared values.

Personal Versus Organizational Values

Your quintessential beliefs exist on two levels—the personal and the organizational. People who make up a church or parachurch organization will have a values set, whether on a conscious or unconscious level, that they bring to their ministry. These are their personal, individual, or private values.

Aspiring church planters would be wise to discover their personal values before they begin a church because their private beliefs will naturally become the organization's public beliefs. When such values are articulated by the church planter, people who share them might be inclined to either join the church or support it financially. People who differ at the values level will look for another church. This approach benefits both parties and eliminates potential problems before they have a chance to develop.

Those who desire to lead an established church, such as Pastor Andy, would also be wise to discover their own personal values first. With these firmly in mind, they are ready to look for a ministry with similar values. This makes for a ministry match that won't result in a divorce after a year or two. I recommend that a pastor and church agree on at least 60 percent of the values before they go to the altar. Anything less places the so-called marriage in serious jeopardy from the start.

Every organization, Christian or secular, has a set of defining precepts. I refer to these as organizational, institutional, or corporate values. I use the word *institution* as a synonym for an organization. I also use the word *corporation* as a synonym for a ministry organization, though it emphasizes the organization as a legal entity. It is correct to use the word *corporation* of the church especially if it has incorporated.

Not only should pastors as leaders be able to articulate their credos, churches should do the same. I recommend that every church have a published credo such as those in appendix B. It will help the church differentiate between their good and bad values so that they can pour their efforts into the former while trying to correct the latter. A published credo will help potential members determine whether they should join this ministry or look for another. It also will assist the church in the selection of a pastor as well as other primary leaders. Their personal values must be in reasonable alignment with the church's.

Actual Versus Aspirational Values

All leaders, as well as their organizations, have both actual and aspirational values. Actual values are those that you own and act upon daily in your ministry. At some time in your life you have embraced them and now they are a part of you. They are intuitive and they naturally manifest themselves as you lead your ministry. When you have to make an organizational decision, they spring into action (whether or not you're aware of them) automatically.

Aspirational values are beliefs that you or your ministry don't own but would like to. Therefore, you don't normally act upon them unless you make a concentrated effort to do so. While actual values represent what is true about you, aspirational values represent what might or could be true about you. My experience has taught me that most pastors do not have the gift of evangelism, and they do not consistently share their faith. This is especially true of those who are seminary graduates who pastor the smaller churches in North America. While all will vote for evangelism, that they aren't doing evangelism on a consistent basis proves that it exists more on the aspirational level than on the actual level.

How can you know which values are real and which are desired? The simple test is to observe your behavior or that of your ministry. If, for example, evangelism is taking place on a consistent basis, then you own that value. If not, then it is aspirational. We know that the Jerusalem Church's values were actual because Luke writes in Acts 2:42 that "they devoted themselves to the apostle's teaching . . . the fellowship . . . the breaking of bread . . . prayer." In short, they practiced what they believed.

Understanding this distinction is important when you attempt to discover and articulate your personal credo or that of your ministry. What you want to discover are your actual values, not your aspirational values. You want to list what is really true of your ministry, not what you hope is true or want to be true in the future. Should you make the mistake of mixing both true and desired values in your credo, then those who observe your ministry will question your integrity. If you say that you value prayer but rarely pray, then you are acting hypocritically.

This raises the question: What do we do with our aspirational values? What if you're a seminary graduate and the pastor of a small church who wants to embrace evangelism as a core value? What if you are attempting to share your faith with the lost on a consistent basis? Aspirational values become part of the mission and strategy of the ministry. They are the things toward which the ministry is striving. They can be listed in a statement separate from the values credo, as a list of values that the church does not yet own, but is working toward.

Single Versus Multiple Values

All ministry organizations as well as leaders have multiple values. If you took time out of your life to list them, they could range from fifty to one hundred and fifty. Again, the core or essential beliefs are those at the top of the list. Some ministries, however, have a single, all-encompassing value that tends to dwarf all the others in the credo.

This is true of your ministry if (1) there is quite a distance between the first-listed value and all the rest, and (2) you ask people what first comes to mind when they think about your ministry and they consistently allude to a single value, such as worship, evangelism, or Bible teaching. Then you know you have a predominate controlling conviction.

Chart 1.2 presents several single values that characterize a number of churches that minister on the North American scene. One is the classroom church whose overriding value is information or, to be more precise, Bible content. When people think about attending the classroom church, their thoughts primarily focus on biblical content. They are drawn to these teaching churches because they want to learn more about the Scriptures.

The critical question is: Are single-value churches good or bad? Is it a good idea to have one overarching value or better to have a balance of beliefs? I believe that this is an issue of biblical balance. God's people need to consume a balanced spiritual diet. To live on dessert alone is not healthy. The problem with the teaching church is that far too often evangelism rarely takes place. And the problem with the evangelistic church is that little teaching takes place. However, both fall under the church's mission according to the Great Commission (Matt. 28:19–20).

What alternative is there for those who attend a single-value church? To gain a balanced diet, they would need to attend a variety of churches

Type of Church	Unifying Value	Role of Pastor	Role of People	Key Emphasis	Typical Tool	Desired Result	Source of Legitimacy	Positive Trait
The Classroom Church	Information	Teacher	Student	To know	Overhead projector	Educated Christian	Expository preaching	Knowledge of Bible
The Soulwinning Church	Evangelism	Evangelist	Bringer	To save	Altar call	Born-again people	Numbers	Heart for lost
The Social-Conscience Church	Justice	Reformer	Recruiter	To care	Petition	Activist	Cause	Compassion for oppressed
The Experiential Church	Experience	Performer	Audience	To Feel	Hand-held mike	Empowerd Christian	Spirit	Vitality
The Family-Reunion Church	Loyalty	Chaplain	Siblings	To belong	Potluck	Secure Christian	Roots	Identity
The Life-Development Church	Character	Coach	Ministry	To be	Ephesians 4	Disciple	Changed lives	Growth

Chart 1.2: Types of American Evangelical Churches

rather than a single church. Last Sunday they attended First Community Church. This Sunday they attended Second Community Church, and next Sunday they plan to attend Third Community. This sounds strangely like a three-ring circus and is not a viable biblical option. The solution is for the single-value church to move quickly toward a healthy, balanced approach.

Congruent Versus Incongruent Values

As a ministry discovers and drafts its credo, it must be careful to look for congruent and incongruent beliefs. Congruent organizational values are those that are harmonious with one another. Like the pieces of a brand new puzzle, they all fit together. Incongruent values contradict one another. They are not harmonious. They affect your ministry subtly— like exchanging a few pieces of one puzzle with a few pieces of another puzzle. You might not be aware that some puzzle parts are missing and that the remaining parts won't fit. If you knew your values weren't harmonious, it's doubtful that you would list them together to begin with.

An example is that of an older established church that desires to preserve all of its traditions of the past while at the same time reaching out to and attracting Generation X. On the one hand, they value their past traditions such as the great hymns of the faith played slowly and quietly on an organ. On the other hand, they value young people and want to do whatever is necessary to draw them in and reach them for Christ. The chances of this happening are slim. The two don't coalesce. This church has some options, however. It could move to two services— the first contemporary and the second traditional—or it could plant a contemporary church designed specifically to target Generation Xers.

Good Values Versus Bad Values

Every ministry, whether church or parachurch, has good and bad values. We'll see in the next chapter that in the values-discovery process you'll unearth both good and bad values. While that might be a little disconcerting, it's a crucial part of the process. In the adventure of discovering our good values, we must also confront our bad values and deal with them accordingly.

What are good values? Good values are essentially God's values. God is their source, and they have everything to do with his truth. How do we know God's truth? The obvious answer is from his Word. Good values are central beliefs that Scripture in some way supports. A knowledge of the Scriptures is requisite to get at them.

The core convictions found in the credos in appendix B are good values. As you peruse them, you'll note that many include a biblical reference for support. I challenge leaders to support their core assumptions with biblical truth; however, we must be careful of proof texting. Biblical integrity insists that the passage actually supports the central value and not simply comes close.

Bad values contradict Scripture in some way. Although you'll not find any of them in the credos in appendix B, the churches represented there do have bad ones. You'll find bad values lurking somewhere in your ministry as well. Some churches such as Lake Country hire the pastor to do the ministry for them. Pastor Andy discovered this after he and the church were already joined. Most often, the pastor's job description includes preaching, teaching, celebrating the ordinances, marrying, burying, soul winning, and so on. The people's job description is to show up on Sunday and drop a tithe in the offering. That's not biblical (Eph. 4:11–16; 1 Corinthians 12; Romans 12) and, therefore, is a bad value.

Often bad values are not articulated but are obvious to those who have been around the ministry for a while. An example would be older, established churches that are determined not to change. For whatever reason, they prefer business as usual. Their motto is: "Come weal or come woe, our status is quo." Consequently, they often keep a trusted group of old-timers in power. They make sure that everyone "colors within the lines." Often you can hear the chairman of the board advise: "If it ain't broke don't fix it."

A summary of the kinds of values that a church or parachurch organization have is provided in chart 1.3.

KINDS OF VALUES		
Conscious	vs.	Unconscious
Shared	vs.	Not Shared
Personal	vs.	Organizational
Actual	vs.	Aspirational
Single	vs.	Multiple
Congruent	vs.	Incongruent
Good	vs.	Bad

Chart 1.3: Kinds of Values

Questions for Thought and Discussion

1. If you are a pastor, do you and your board disagree on many issues? If you are a board member, do you disagree a lot with your pastor? If you answered yes to either question, how would you explain your disagreements? What do you plan to do about this?

2. Are you convinced that your core values are important? Can you think of any other reasons why they are important that aren't mentioned in this book? If yes, what?

3. What is the difference between your values and your mission? Your vision? Your strategy? Your doctrinal statement? Have you confused any of these?

4. As you examine your core beliefs, have they remained constant over the years? Have any changed? If they have, when? Do you anticipate this happening in the future?

5. What, if anything, are you passionate about? What does passion have to do with your personal beliefs?

6. Are your core values biblical? Can you cite a passage of Scripture that supports your values? If not, why not?

7. Do your beliefs drive your ministry? If so, how? What kind of impact do they exert on your decisions, goals, finances? Were you aware of this prior to reading this book?

8. Are most of your values or those of your ministry held at a conscious or unconscious level? Do you and your board share many of your values? How has this affected you and the ministry?

9. Are your values mostly aspirational or actual? What's the difference? Do you sense that a single value predominates over your church? If so, what is it? Do you suspect that either you or your ministry has some bad values? Name one.

Notes

1. Lynne Hybels and Bill Hybels, *Rediscovering Church* (Grand Rapids: Zondervan, 1995), 153.
2. Bill Gates, *The Road Ahead* (New York: Viking, 1995), 9.
3. From Alan Perkins. Used by permission.
4. Hybels, *Rediscovering Church*, 191.
5. James M. Kouzes and Barry Z. Posner, *The Leadership Challenge* (San Francisco: Jossey Bass, 1987), 193.

2

The Discovery of Core Values
What Is Your Credo?

Pastor Andy believed that as soon as he pulled the covers over his weary body he would instantly fall asleep. He was fatigued to the bone. He had worked out vigorously at the local YMCA before his meeting with the board. Also, the long difficult evening with the members had sapped his strength emotionally.

He was wrong. He found it impossible to fall asleep. The events of the evening, the words that had been said, and the disapproving looks on the faces all served together as a stimulant—an emotional cup of coffee—to keep him awake. Numerous questions took turns cycling through his weary mind. As the sleepless night wore on, he tossed and turned and asked himself: *Did the meeting have to go that way? What could I have done or said differently? Is Harry Smith trying to run me off? Why didn't the seminary better prepare me for this situation? Why was my preparation so academic? Is it fair to blame the seminary? Do I have what it takes to lead a church? What should I do in an attempt to resolve this problem? Is it time to leave this church?*

Of all these questions, the most immediate is the next to the last one: What should I do in an attempt to resolve this problem? It has a direct bearing on the last question. We discovered in the last chapter that a significant part of the problem is core values—both Andy's and the board's. While core values aren't the only factor at Lake Country Church, they are significant and must be addressed. If Pastor Andy and his board knew their central beliefs, then they would understand to a great degree why they so rarely agree on the direction of the church. Then Andy would be able to answer his last question as well: whether or not it was time to leave Lake Country Church.

The focus of part 1 of this book is the discovery of personal and corporate values. Leaders, whether professional staff or lay board members, have their own core set of organizational values. Leaders will greatly enhance their ministry and save themselves much pain if they discover and articulate their personal values first. The preparation of leaders whether in churches, Bible or Christian colleges, and seminaries should include the discovery and formation of each leader's set of fundamental values.

The ministry itself will have a corporate values set. The church or parachurch organization should discover and communicate through a credo the values that drive it as a ministry. A credo serves to define the ministry of a church and communicate to all what it's about, providing the ministry's distinctive "up front" so that potential members may determine if that is the place for them. The organizations or subministries such as Christian education, worship, and so on that make up the broader ministry will also have organizational values. Subministry values must be congruent and under the umbrella of the organization's values set. For example, if the church values creativity and innovation, then the subministries should value the same.

Suppose the seminary that Andy attended had carefully taught its pastoral students the ministry ABCs, including the concept of core organizational values. Assume that a required course had taught all aspiring pastors to discover their values and then had taught them how to discover those of their prospective churches. What would that course be like? The values-discovery process consists of at least three steps: (1) determining who discovers the ministry's values; (2) deciding or discovering which values to unearth (using the values audit); and (3) learning how to resolve values differences.

Who Discovers the Ministry's Values?

The first step is to determine who is involved in the discovery process. The ideal is to have everyone who is associated with the ministry involved. Since this isn't feasible, the responsibility rests with the primary leadership. In the church, this would be the head pastor, any staff, and the church board. In the parachurch ministry, this would be a president or general director, and the ministry board. In the marketplace, it would be the president, CEO, and the corporate board.

Most people, even good leaders, desire to be led in some way. Regardless of the environment—spiritual, military, or political—people look for leaders with character. They look for men and women who cast a significant vision for their people and define what's really important to the establishment. One of the important contributions that leaders make to their organizations is to discover, communicate, implement, and enforce the central corporate beliefs. Regardless of who actually discovers the values, the leadership is responsible to see that values discovery takes place.

Although primary leaders are responsible, they must not attempt the process alone. The characteristic of a great leader is that he or she is able to involve others in the action. If the organization is a church, then the size of the church will dictate who is involved and to what degree (see figure 2.1). The sheer size of a large church means that fewer people are involved in the values-discovery process. This would include those on the staff and board along with lay leaders of certain vital ministries in the church. People in large churches sense that due to the ministry's size not everyone can have their say. Consequently, they're more dependent on those at a higher level of leadership.

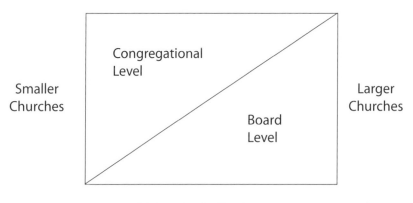

Figure 2.1: Levels of Involvement

In a smaller church more people may take an active part in the process, which begins with the pastor and the board and includes other leaders ranging from Sunday school teachers to small-group leaders. At Lake Country Church, this would comprise Pastor Andy, his board, input from the Sunday school teachers, and a few other key people. The problem in the smaller church is that the "squeaky wheels" who often represent special interests have a louder voice than in a larger ministry. Consequently, it takes strong, skillful leadership to protect the church from their undue influence.

How Do You Decide or Discover the Ministry's Values?

The way that you discover your ministry organization's fundamental beliefs is by conducting a values audit. Its purpose is not to create or shape the values but to discover those that are already in place and currently driving the ministry, whether good or bad. Thus, the focus is on actual not aspirational values. Should the ministry mistakenly articulate its aspirational values, then its people will question the credibility of the institution and its leadership. They will examine the value and protest, "We don't believe that!"

Since a ministry's defining values exist at two levels—the personal and the congregational—you will need to audit both levels. It is best that you start with your personal values, then move to the values of the ministry institution that you serve or hope to serve. This exercise is mandatory for church boards as well as for pastors and their staffs. The same is true for those in similar positions in parachurch ministries. Students preparing for ministry should discover not only their personal beliefs but also know how to unearth those of a prospective ministry.

Auditing Personal Beliefs

Several ways exist for you to audit your personal precepts. You may pursue one or even better a combination of the following.

Write them down on a piece of paper. The assumption is that you know what a value is. If not, then look briefly at a sample credo or two in appendix B. I use the term *briefly* because you don't want another organization's credo to unduly influence the process. Initially, you may write several sentences in an attempt to capture the value. The goal, however, is brevity because it leads to clarity. The simplest approach is to write a statement such as: I value relevant Bible exposition. The temptation will be to say much more. Instead, use one of the following shortened forms.

I value _____ .
I believe _____ .
I commit to _____ .

If you must say more, then place your explanation below the initial belief statement. The credo of Lakeview Community Church of Cedar Hill, Texas, provides an example of how to do this (see appendix B).

Review the credos of several churches, looking for a common cause. For example, you might look over the beliefs in the credos found in appendix B.[1] Some will figuratively "jump off the page" at you—they are your personal values. You will feel an affinity with them. They will attract your attention, and you will experience a sense of common cause. Write these down. You must focus on your actual values as well as your aspirational values. At this point in the process, the purpose of the audit is to discover what you believe, not what you should believe.

Take the Personal Core Values Audit in appendix C. This audit is sufficiently broad to include the values of both church and parachurch organizations. As you and those in your ministry look over the beliefs listed in this audit, certain ones should grab your attention. Again, as in the paragraph above, you will feel an affinity with some but not with others. Rate the values from 1 (the lowest) to 5 (the highest). There is also a place for you to add any values that you might own that aren't on the list. The ones you've rated as a 4 or 5 are your core values. Prioritize those with the highest scores. If you have more than ten, then choose the top ten.

Describe what to you is an ideal ministry. The question is: If God were to give you a perfect ministry, what would it look like? If you're a pastor, what for you would be the perfect church. Would you have a staff? How many people would be on staff? What would they do? Describe the perfect board. What kind of worship would you have? What programs would you implement? What kind of sermons would you preach? All the above are associated with values. For example, the first question about staff concerns whether you value team ministry. Bring those values to the surface, identify them, and place them in your credo.

Auditing Corporate Beliefs

Several techniques are available for auditing a church or parachurch ministry's core organizational values. The first three will help prospective leaders know in advance a ministry's beliefs if they are not articulated or known. The third and fourth will help a ministry discover its own beliefs.

Request that the ministry provide a copy of its credo. This is for those who aspire to serve the ministry in some way as leader, staff, or volunteer. One of the reasons I wrote *Values-Driven Leadership* was to call attention to the need for ministries to discover and articulate their God-honoring beliefs. I have observed that more ministries are developing credos. It shouldn't surprise you, however, if the ministry you're interested in doesn't have one or doesn't even know what you're requesting. This is still a relatively new concept, though it's a ministry basic.

Articulate a ministry's values based on your personal observation. This requires that you visit the ministry or have some involvement in it. For example, when you attend a church service, you can discern a number of the church's values by skillful observation. When you approach the church, you should note if the facilities are well maintained and if the grounds are properly kept. Once inside the facility, are there signs of poor maintenance? Is there a sense of excitement and enthusiasm among the attendees? Is the worship planned and performed well? What is the sermon about and did people respond? If it's a Baptist church, inquire about the number of baptisms—you'll get a feel for its passion toward evangelism.

Use the Corporate Core Values Audit in appendix D. I have designed it to help ministries unearth their beliefs. It will accomplish the same for those who desire to know a ministry's values before identifying with the organization. Lake Country Church could have used it to discover their values in order to list them in a church credo. They could have mailed this to potential pastor Andy before any courtship. Had he known, Pastor Andy could have used this audit during their engagement to determine if there should have been a marriage with Lake Country Church. Not having done this, both Andy and the church are now facing the possibility of a painful divorce. Every leader and every ministry should use their courtship as a time to discern their value alignment.

The Corporate Core Values Audit focuses on three specific areas that serve to quickly get at an organization's vital underpinnings. The areas are time, treasures, and talents. Regardless of the organization, people value their time because not many have much discretionary time. Most of us are busy people who are good at filling up our calendars with what we believe are important events. I put time before treasure because a growing number of people are more willing to pay to have some things accomplished than to take personal time to do them. As for talent, highly talented people tend not to invest their talents where things are done poorly. Good talent attracts other good talent; poor talent draws poor talent. Consequently, the audit seeks to determine where people invest their time, treasure, and talent in the organization.

Gather the ministry team and discover common values together. While gathering the entire team is preferable, it's also possible to gather different groups in the organization on different days. This works for both large and small ministries. CAM International, an independent missions organization located in Dallas, Texas, used this process at one of their annual convocations, which involved approximately 250 missionaries.

Begin the process by breaking the organization up into work teams of five to ten people. Either assign or ask each team to determine a leader to facilitate discussion and a recorder to take notes. Ask each group to brainstorm and determine what they believe are the ministry's key driving beliefs. They may list as many as they want. You might show them several examples to help catalyze the process. Remind them that a good value is biblical, passionate, shared, constant, clear, implementable, and congruent with all the others.

Once the groups have composed their lists, require them to eliminate all but their top ten values. Then bring the groups together and list the values on a white board, overhead projector, bulletin board, cork board (using a storyboard approach), or some other means. Eliminate those that are essentially the same though worded differently. Then ask the group to interact and narrow the remaining ones to no more than ten. It's okay to have eleven or twelve if they can't agree on ten.

Using a storyboard approach works with most groups. Once you have taught what values are and have shown several credos, ask the team to identify what they think their ministry's values are. This process involves one or two recorders who write the values on 5x8-inch cards, using a black marker. Next, put removable poster Scotch tape (both sides are sticky) on the back of the cards and place them on the wall or some other appropriate place where all can see them. Once all the values are up, give each participant ten red coding labels. Have them place these on what they believe are the ten most important values. The ten values that get the most red labels are the ministry's core values.

There are three advantages to discovering common values together. First, it's a bottom-up process as well as a top-down process. People at the grassroots level have a say as well as do the leaders at the top. Second, with everyone taking part in the process, all will get their fingerprints on the credo. This results in a ministry-wide ownership in the final product. Each person senses that he or she played a major part in determining the credo—these values are my values! Finally, because they have ownership and a sense of common cause, the chances are better that the people will live and minister by the values.

Comparing and Interpreting the Audit Results

Once you've completed the values-discovery process, the question becomes, What do you do with the results? First, the individual and the organization will know its values and be able to develop a credo statement (the topic of the next chapter). We understood this going into the process. The ministry, however, can use the results when looking for a new leader, staff member, or volunteer, to search for common cause and build their leadership teams.

Comparison and interpretation are how you go about accomplishing this. Once you have discovered the values of the potential team members, then you compare them to the values of the ministry to determine if a ministry match exists. The ideal is to share all the same values. Since this isn't likely, even in a church or parachurch ministry, you'll need to look for common cause.

Pastor Andy and the board of Lake Country Church could have used the audits to discover their personal and corporate credos. The next step would have been to compare the two and interpret the results, determining common cause. If both potential pastor and board had ten core values, then common cause asks: How many values do they share? In the process of comparing their beliefs, they might have discovered that they shared only three. This means that they agree on 30 percent of what is at the core. The bar graph in figure 2.2 represents this agreement.

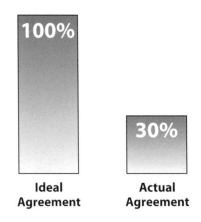

Figure 2.2: Common Cause—30% Agreement

What does this mean for the ministry? How will it affect the working and leading relationships of the pastor and board? The general interpretation is that over several years of ministry they will likely agree on 30 percent of their decisions and disagree on 70 percent. Of course, the particular key beliefs at issue would temper this. It's possible that a number of ministry decisions involve mostly the 30 percent where consensus exists. This means that they would agree much of the time, but don't count on it. The chances are even better that those ministry decisions would involve the 70 percent where they disagree. Thus, they would be at odds on practically everything of import.

The process could also be reversed. The pastor and the board might agree on 70 percent of their values and differ on only 30 percent as depicted in figure 2.3. The chances of a successful relationship have increased significantly. What is the best ratio for actual agreement? The answer depends on the board and the leader. Some can tolerate more disagreement than others. Some leaders have a proven track record as change agents. In general, I believe that agreement on six or more beliefs is necessary for a good partnership. One factor that influences this is whether the ministry is growing, has leveled off, or is dying. Sometimes a dying ministry is willing to make changes that a growing or leveled off one isn't. Another influencing factor is the values themselves. Some are of such importance that they alone will affect common cause. One is the ministry's position on the Scriptures. Does the Bible direct all that we do, or does something else? A second is creativity versus tradition. Does this church value the traditions of its past, or is it ready for change and the creation of new traditions?

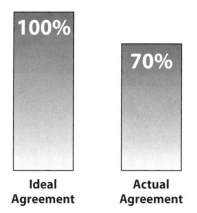

Figure 2.3: Common Cause—70% Agreement

How to Resolve Values Differences

This chapter is all about how to discover personal and corporate organizational values. The goal is that both the leaders and ministry organizations know their core beliefs and articulate the same in a credo. But what happens when all have accomplished this and discover moderate to significant differences? If Pastor Andy and his board complete the values-discovery process and create a credo, they will find themselves in strong disagreement. What should they do?

One solution is to ignore these differences. Leaders do so to their peril, however. The differences are like dry tender, waiting for a lightening spark or a carelessly discarded match to ignite them. The North American church terrain is strewn with the empty shells of charred buildings that belong to those who chose to ignore their values differences.

The answer and best solution is to pursue the value-resolution process. This was the response of the leadership of the early church in Acts 6:1–7 when the Grecian Jews complained that the Hebraic Jews were overlooking their widows in the distribution of food. The Twelve chose not to ignore the problem and God honored their efforts.

What is involved in the values-resolution process? I suggest the following six steps. First, bathe the entire process and all the people involved in prayer. James says, "You do not have, because you do not ask God" (James 4:2). Pray specifically about your differences. James also says, "The prayer of a righteous man is powerful and effective" (James 5:16). Ask those involved in the resolution process to pray together. Allow God to do his work with his people.

Second, study the Scriptures together. Hebrews 4:12 says that God's Word can penetrate the hearts of people as well as penetrate to the heart of an issue. As you study together, ask the basic nuts and bolts questions:

Why are we here? Why do we do what we do? What are we doing? What are we supposed to be doing? How do we accomplish the ministry? Scripture answers these questions and more and, in the process, addresses the issues of the heart, personality differences, and most importantly, disparate values.

Third, be bold enough to acknowledge your differences and discuss them together. Conflict isn't new to the church—it has been a constant since the early church (Acts 5:1–10; 6:1–7; 15:1–21, 36–41). The early church's procedure was not to ignore or cover up their problems. Instead, they acknowledged them openly, discussed them together, and reached a resolution. We must take time to discuss our differences with one another and carefully listen to one another with a view toward resolution.

Fourth, pursue consensus not compromise. Most often people resolve their differences by compromising their positions. The idea is that everyone gives a little so that we can solve our problems and all can go home happy. Reality is that compromise rarely satisfies anyone and resolves few problems. Instead, people should agree to disagree. Then they must state what they believe and defend their positions. This is what took place at the Jerusalem Council in Acts 15. Normally, those who get the most votes win, but consensus says that the others agree to go along with them. If this isn't possible, then they're free to move on as Paul and Barnabas chose to do as described in Acts 15:36–41. The only restriction is that they not demean others in the process.

Fifth, it may be wise to work with an intermediary or consultant. This would likely involve spending money, but the results could be worth every penny and more. Some believe that the leader or pastor should function in this role. My experience is that few pastors are trained in or understand conflict resolution—most function as "prophets without honor" in their churches. The presence of an intermediary or consultant would disarm personal attacks, jettison much personal baggage, and keep the discussions focused on the issues. If the outside person is not able to help, this would be a sign that the ministry is in serious trouble and either needs a new board or a new leader.

Sixth, whatever the situation, there's a point where leaders must lead. The adage that you can't keep all the people happy all the time is true. Some pastors want to be liked and often fall into the trap of attempting to keep everyone in the church happy. Most lay boards are notorious for this—some view it as their primary function. The result is that there are both anemic leadership and unhappy congregants. In particular, those who know how to manipulate these pastors and boards will make a point of always being unhappy and use this to pursue their agendas for the ministry. Leaders must pursue the truth in love. This often means doing what is right and suffering the consequences. That's the price for being a leader. If the ministry can't live with that, then it's time for the leader to look for a new ministry. If the leader can't live with that, then he or she might not be a leader.

Questions for Thought and Discussion

1. Are you convinced that you need to discover your core values or those of the ministry you work with? Why or why not?
2. Are you currently going through a values-formation period? If so, what are the circumstances? If you aren't, can you recall such a time in the past? What effect might such a time have on you or your ministry?
3. Who in your ministry is responsible for discovering the core organizational values? Did you include the point person? Did you include the key decision makers? Where are you in the process?
4. What are the core beliefs of the point person? Any bad ones? What are they? What are the core beliefs of the organization that he or she serves? Any bad ones? What are they? Does the board agree among themselves on the ministry's essential values? Why or why not?
5. Does the leader of the ministry and the board differ on any values? If so, what are they? If you are the leader, how much actual agreement is necessary for you to take a ministry or remain in a ministry?
6. If you're the leader and you don't agree with your board on the ministry's essential precepts, what do you plan to do about it? If you're part of a board and you as a group don't agree with one another, what will you do about it? What if you don't agree as a board with the leader, what will you do about it?

Notes

1. For a more extensive list of potential values, see the various credos in the appendices of my book *Values-Driven Leadership* (Grand Rapids: Baker, 1996).

3

The Development of Core Values

How to Construct Your Credo

Pastor Andy placed a bookmark between the pages of his book to mark where he had just finished reading. He laid the book on his cluttered desk, slumped back in his chair, and began to reflect on what he'd just read. A friend and fellow pastor had mailed him a package that included a short, handwritten letter updating the progress of his church in Seattle. It was growing and a number of people had come to faith in Christ. Andy had to admit that he was envious of his friend's success.

Included with the letter was a book on ministry basics written by one of the professors from the seminary they had both attended, who had taught in the area of pastoral ministries. Andy had been too busy taking various required courses to find time to sit in any of this man's classes. He, like many other seminarians, believed that "you could get all that stuff later when in ministry." In the postscript at the end of his letter, his friend had succinctly written, "You've *got* to read this one!"

The first part of the book included a section on organizational core values. Andy couldn't put it down. As he completed the first chapter, he realized that a major reason why he and his board were having so much difficulty was because of differing beliefs. He felt as if he'd been groping in the dark, and the author had turned on a bright light for him. All of a sudden he could see! When he finished the second chapter, he turned to the appendix and took the Personal Core Values Audit for himself and the Corporate Core Values Audit for the church. He and the church shared only 30 percent common cause.

He had just finished reading the third chapter on the development of a values statement or credo. As he sat and reflected, he decided that he would order a copy of the book for each of his board members and ask them to read it. Meanwhile, he would attempt to write a credo for their church. It would be a good exercise and might help him and the board resolve some of their differences.

How should Pastor Andy develop a statement of core values? What's involved in drafting a credo for a ministry? The answer is threefold. There exists a preparation phase, a process phase, and a determination phase.

The Preparation for Drafting Your Credo

Constructing a building has some things in common with constructing a beliefs statement. One is that both require some preparation before the process begins. The preparation for credo construction is deciding who develops the credo, the values that make up its credo, and the reasons why they should write the values down.

The Contractor of the Credo

Who is responsible for the construction of a ministry's credo? Just as the leadership is responsible to discover the values (see chapter 2), so it's responsible to develop the credo. When it's time to get something done, most look to their leaders for direction. In the church, this is the pastoral team and the board. Both Pastor Andy and his board should see that the church develops a values statement that is tailor-made for itself. In the parachurch ministry, it's the point leader, such as the president or director, and the board who are responsible.

Shaping a ministry's defining beliefs, however, is preeminently the responsibility of the point person for the organization. The values that characterize most established organizations have also characterized their leaders. This has proved true in the marketplace with such individuals as Ross Perot, formerly of EDS, Bill Gates of Microsoft, and Sam Walton of Wal-Mart. It is also true of Christian organizations led by individuals, such as James Dobson with Focus on the Family, Bill Bright with Campus Crusade, and Lorne Saney of the Navigators.

In an entrepreneurial venture such as those above or that of the church, the core beliefs are those of the point person. Then he or she invites others with similar beliefs to join the venture. In an established work, the point person must consider the views of the board and the people before he or she joins them. The primary leader brings key beliefs to the ministry, and the ministry already owns a set of critical values. This can be problematic, and if there exist substantial differences, I suggest that the potential leader not join the ministry. The other option is to attempt to change the ministry significantly or attempt to change one's own values. Either option, while possible, isn't promising.

The wise leader of an established ministry invites those in the ministry to join him or her in the values-development process. The size of a larger ministry such as a church of three hundred or more will limit lay involvement. The smaller ministry can expect more participation (see figure 2.1). One option is to develop an initial ministry credo, then present it to a limited number of key lay leaders, giving them permission to change, add to, or approve it. I suggest that you use someone with language skills and creativity, such as a writer or teacher, to go over the document. Ask them to review and fine-tune the product; however, you don't want them to tamper with the actual values. Instead, they are to work only with the wording. They may need to word or reword the document in relevant, contemporary language that will communicate to those in the third millennium. The credos in appendix B provide examples that have gone through this process.

The Contractor's Building Blocks

Contractors don't create out of nothing—that is God's privilege alone. Contractors have to work with existing material; so do constructors of credos. The building blocks of the construction industry are wood, metal, cement, and so on. The building blocks of the ministry are the core organizational values. In particular, these values are the ones discovered in the values-discovery phase. At this point, most organizational values are like the house that the contractor has erected but has not finished. The walls are up and the roof is in place, but the facility is in need of paint and all the trim work.

You must remember throughout the process that you are working with the actual, not the aspirational, values. Again, an astute ministry constituency may view a ministry credo that consists primarily of aspirational values as hypocritical. But what does the established church that wants to be evangelistic but isn't there yet do with these aspirations? Can they put evangelism in their credo?

These values can be put in the credo if they are somehow marked as aspirational. For example, you could place an asterisk beside them and note somewhere within the document what the asterisk represents. Another solution is to place the actual values together in one list and the desired (aspirational) values together in another. In the former, you could say that you value or are committed to the following beliefs. In the latter, you might say that you aspire to or are becoming an organization that values these beliefs.

The Contractor's Blueprints

A contractor must have a written plan. It's called a blueprint. If he doesn't write down his plans, the result won't be a building or a house—

it will be chaos. Credo contractors also must have a written plan. Written values clarify precisely what you believe. Writing forces you to think and be specific. If you know what your values are, you should be able to put them on a piece of paper. If you can't do that, then you need to do some more work in the values-identification and values-clarification phases.

Written values place the authority of the leadership behind the credo. Core beliefs are a statement by the leadership of what the ministry values. Communicating them orally leaves room for noncompliance; communicating them in writing makes them official. When the leadership of the ministry pens the organization's values in ink, no one can plead ignorance should they violate those values. Thus, the leadership can enforce compliance from those who choose to ignore the values or who operate with a different set of beliefs.

Numerous ways exist to communicate values—the life and example of the leadership, a message or sermon, storytelling, visual images, the ministry's language and metaphors, a brochure, what the ministry celebrates, and who its heroes are. A written statement, however, is a vital first step in the values-casting process. By writing, you put flesh on what may otherwise be sparse, abstract ideas. This allows them to spring to life in a fresh way that adds meaning and has impact on people's lives. In addition, a written credo will save you countless hours of explanation. People can first read what you value, then ask questions for clarification.

The Process of Drafting Your Credo

Once the foundation is laid, you are ready to construct your values statement. The process consists of three steps: determining the number of values, the actual values, and the values format.

Determining the Number of Values

The first step is to determine the number of values that will make up the credo. Answer the question: How many beliefs should I have in my statement? Since the average leader will have from fifty to as many as one hundred core beliefs, how many should he or she include in a personal credo or that of the ministry organization?

A survey of the various credos for churches, parachurch ministries, and marketplace organizations reveals that values range in number from one to seventeen. In general, the marketplace organizations had the fewest. This is because they have been wrestling with these issues and asking these questions much longer than most churches. Hewlett-Packard is a business with only one driving belief: "The HP way says, 'Do unto others as you would have them do unto you.' That's really what it's all about."[1] Ken Blanchard, a Christian and president of Blanchard Training and Development has three: doing things right, building mutually satisfying partnerships, and accomplishing the company goals.[2] Two ministry organizations had the most values. CAM International, an independent missions organization, has fifteen. Saddleback Valley Community Church, a Southern Baptist church located in Orange County, California, has seventeen (see appendix B). The rest hovered somewhere between five and ten core beliefs. In *Built to Last*, Collins and Porras note that visionary companies have from three to six.[3]

An important question is: What is core? The Jerusalem Church included at least six things. Anything less than that would seem to leave out certain biblical essentials. With the exception of some churches, more than ten might indicate that they are not down to their core values, and may only serve to confuse people and frustrate their efforts.

The final verdict as to the number of essentials lies with both the leadership and the individuals who make up the organization and should be decided by consensus and not compromise. If, however, people insist on fewer than five or more than ten, then that's the proper number for the ministry. The final verdict rests with the leadership, those who are responsible to see that the ministry accomplishes its mission, and the constituency, those who are responsible to carry out that mission. The leadership and the missionaries of CAM International opted for fifteen. Any number less than fifteen left out what they believed were essentials.

Once you have settled on the number of values, you may wish to arrange them in your credo in order of priority. This says something about the most important of the important. That is why many organizations begin with a statement about the Scriptures and their commitment to them. The Bible is foundational to all the values that make up the credo.

In some situations, you might list them out of priority. You might feel that helping your people remember the values is more important than arranging them in order of importance. Consequently, you might form the credo around an acrostic. This involves taking the first letter of each value to form a memorable word such as the name of the ministry. For example, you will find the credo of Lakeview Community Church in appendix B. If it had eight values rather than seven, they could attempt to fashion each around the word *Lakeview*. The *L* could stand for lay ministry, the *A* for an active prayer ministry, and so on (see figure 3.1). While this would help people remember the church's credo, it could also seem contrived. The ministry leadership, with the advice of the ministry constituency, will need to make this decision.

L ay Ministry

A ctive Prayer

K ingdom Growth

E xposition of the Scriptures

V ital Community

I nnovation and Creativity

E xcellence

W orship

Figure 3.1: Sample Acrostic Credo

Another option is to list your ministry's primary values and secondary values. The primary values consist of the core or top-ten values (or whatever number you determine). The secondary values are also important precepts to the ministry but not as important as the primary ones. The two lists help you bring to the surface more of the values that affect your ministry. This is ideal for ministries that find numerous values and have some trouble in limiting them to ten. You are then able to place more of them before the leadership team or your people while separating what is most important.

Determine the Actual Values

The second step in developing the credo is to determine whether the beliefs on your list are values or something else. The reason for this step is that some values are often confused with the form that a value may take. An example is found in the credo of Lakeview Community Church of Cedar Hill, Texas (see appendix B). They have listed small groups as their fourth value.

A Commitment to Small Groups
We are committed to small-group ministry as one of the most effective means of building relationships, stimulating spiritual growth, and developing leaders.

The problem is that a small group is a form that a value takes and not the value itself. Every value has at least one form that implements it. A small group is the form that implements a value, such as authentic biblical community. Other values are evangelism, worship, prayer, teaching, and so on. All of these can take place in the context of a small group. Other values take other forms (see chart 3.1).

VALUE	FORM
Authentic community	small group
Evangelism	crusade
Fellowship	potluck meal
Scripture	exposition

Chart 3.1: Forms of Values

The question is: How do you separate the two? How do you know which is the value and which is the form? There are two ways.

The first is to ask: Is this an end or a means to an end? The value is the end; the form is the means to an end. While values do have a greater end (to glorify God), in a sense they are an end in themselves. This is true of the values in chart 3.1 above. The forms that they take are a means to accomplish them. Therefore, if we ask: Is our small-groups program and end in itself? the answer is no. The groups are a means to an end such as an authentic biblical community. The same is true for conducting city-wide crusades. Here we would ask: Are we conducting these crusades as an end in themselves, simply to be putting on crusades? Or, are they the means to a greater end—evangelism?

The second is to ask: Why are we doing what we are doing? What you or your ministry are doing isn't the value. The reason you're doing it is the value. The *what* question brings to the surface the forms that serve to realize your values. The *why* question identifies your central values. Your church may be sponsoring a potluck meal once a month after church. That's the *what* or the *form*. The reason for the potluck meal is for fellowship.

Why is it so important to distinguish between the values and their forms? One reason is that the values, on the one hand, are timeless and should never change. The values that were important to the church in the first century are just as important to the church in the twenty-first century. They have not changed at all. Therefore, evangelism or worship is just as important today as in biblical times. On the other hand, the forms that the values take are timely. Scripture doesn't appear to hold any forms as sacrosanct. They can and should change from culture to culture and time to time because this is how the church or any other ministry remains relevant to the culture that it's trying to reach.

If leaders and their ministries wish to stay current and relate relevantly to the culture in which they desire to have an impact, they must regularly evaluate the forms and the programs that the values are expressed in to see if they are still having an impact. Value forms can grow stale and lose their ministry punch. When this happens, the ministry must change them or risk not having an effective ministry. Often the ministry will include the forms along with their values in the credo. This means that the credo will undergo some change when the ministry changes or adds a new form or method.

Determining the Values Format

A values format is the form that the values take when expressed in the credo. It includes the precise words, phrases, clauses, sentence structure, and other elements that communicate the organization's beliefs. There is no one correct values format that fits every church or parachurch ministry. Each ministry has to determine and develop one that best fits its culture and serves its people well. A review of the credos in appendix B and the Acadiana Community Church credo in appendix A demonstrates the different approaches that various ministries use to express their beliefs. These may prove to be most helpful as you consider developing your own credo. As we look at some of them, you might find a form that fits your ministry context well.

Acadiana Community Church

Acadiana Community Church is a recently planted church located in a community north of New Orleans, Louisiana. Their credo is located in appendix A, and it consists of eight core values. The first is representative of how the church has crafted the entire credo.

We Value Full Devotion to Christ and His Cause
We believe that whole-hearted devotion to Jesus Christ is not only the biblical norm for the believer, but that anything less is sin in God's eyes. Full devotion should be expected of and encouraged by every believer in the community.

They begin with a lead statement that identifies each value. It takes the form of a concise, well-worded sentence. This is followed by a one, two, or more sentence explanation of the value. The last value—servant leadership—has seven sentences. Several also go on to state how the ministry will apply the value, or what the church expects of those who become a part of it. Thus, Acadiana expects and encourages their church community to be fully devoted to Christ.

Fellowship Bible Church-Dallas

Fellowship Bible Church-Dallas is located in Dallas, Texas. It is popularly known as FBC-Dallas. The reason they have placed Dallas in the name is that the church is one of many fellowship Bible churches located in the Dallas metropolis. Gene Getz either planted or encouraged the planting of these churches, and many use a designation to differentiate them from one another. Their credo (and the rest that follow) is found in appendix B and consists of ten core values. Each begins with a caption followed by a colon and then an explanation of the belief. The following is the third in their statement:

Grace-Oriented
We emphasize God's unconditional acceptance and full forgiveness through Jesus Christ. We attempt to motivate people through love and thankfulness rather than guilt, shame, and duty.

All the captions except the last consist of only two words. Most of the explanations contain two or, at the most, three sentences. In addition, the explanations state how the church applies the values to the church. A quick review of the applications reveals the following phrases: *we attempt to*, *we desire*, *we emphasize*, *we seek*, *we stress*, and others.

Lakeview Community Church
Lakeview Community Church is located in Cedar Hill, Texas, a suburb southeast of Dallas, Texas. Their beliefs statement is similar to those of Acadiana and FBC-Dallas. The first value reflects the role that the Scriptures play in their church.

A Commitment to Relevant Bible Exposition
We believe that the Bible is God's inspired Word, the authoritative and trustworthy rule of faith and practice for Christians. The Bible is both timeless and timely, relevant to the common needs of all people at all times and to the specific problems of contemporary living. Therefore, we are committed to equipping Christians, through the preaching and teaching of God's word, to follow in every sphere of life.

They lead with a caption that is longer than that of FBC-Dallas and that includes the word *commitment*. It's followed with an explanation of the value and an application. The latter is signaled in several instances by the word *therefore*. What is different about their statements is that they support several of them with Scripture. The second value is a commitment to prayer that includes Matthew 7:7–11 and James 5:13–18. This approach serves to give the support of Scripture to the values that include them.

Saddleback Valley Community Church
Saddleback Valley Community Church is located in Mission Viejo, California, just south of Los Angeles. Like Lakeview Community Church, their first value reflects the place of Scripture in the church.

We Value the Application of Scripture

"Do not merely listen to the Word, and so deceive yourselves. Do what it says" (James 1:22).

This church begins with a sentence that clearly identifies the value. Rather than follow with an explanation, the credo continues to sight various passages of Scripture from different translations that support the value. In some cases a value may include as many as five passages as in their fourth value—feedback.

Willow Creek Community Church

Willow Creek Community Church is located in Barrington, Illinois, a suburb west of Chicago, Illinois. One of the largest churches in America, the ministry team has crafted ten core values. The following is the first value and is representative of all ten:

We believe that anointed teaching is the catalyst for transformation in individuals' lives and in the church.

This value includes the concept of teaching for life change as found in Romans 12:7; 2 Timothy 3:16–17; and James 1:23–25. Willow Creek has opted not to introduce each value with a caption but to move immediately into a sentence statement. Though not as obvious as those of Saddleback, the values are found in each sentence statement. The first is individual life change; the second, people; the third, cultural relevance; the fourth, authenticity; and so on. The church has worded the sentences so that they include not only the value but the application of the value to the community. Hence, anointed teaching will accomplish individual life change. Willow Creek has also chosen to follow each sentence with various key concepts and several biblical passages in support of each.

Wooddale Church

Wooddale Church is located in Eden Prairie, Minnesota, near St. Paul. Their credo consists of seven vital values. The first calls the reader's attention to God.

God-Centered

Wooddale Church exists for God. In every person and program God is first, God is experienced, and God is pleased. We delight to constantly have God on our minds and in our conversations. Wooddale Church is the people and place where God is experienced. Public gathering to worship is a primary expression. Personal godly living is an equally important expression.

All of Wooddale's values are introduced with a caption containing a concise statement of the specific belief. As with Saddleback and some of the others, there is no doubt what the values are. All but one are followed with a hyphen and some kind of qualifier: God-centered, Bible-based, outreach-oriented, disciple-making, and others. Several sentences accompany each value caption and provide further explanation. The leadership has also articulated these sentences in an application format that answers the question: So what?

Now the important question is: Are any of these credos helpful to you in determining the best values format for your church? In working with various ministries, I have noted that a particular format will seem to jump off the page at the values developer or values development team. Others prefer an eclectic approach that uses a portion from each statement to come up with one that is unique to them.

Questions for Thought, Discussion, and Application

1. Who in your ministry is responsible for crafting the credo? Is it the point person or primary leader? Are others involved in the process?
2. Are your values aspirational or actual? What is the difference? Will you include both in your credo? If yes, how will you do this to avoid confusing the two?
3. In constructing your credo, have you written your beliefs down? Why or why not? What are some reasons for writing them down?
4. How many values have you included in your credo? Why this number? Are they core? If you have more than ten, are there any you could drop? Are they listed in order of priority? Is this helpful or not? Would it help in communicating your core values to list them in an acrostic?
5. Have you checked your credo for any so-called values that are actually forms? What is the difference? Did you find any? What did you do about them?
6. Did you find any of the credos in appendices A or B helpful in crafting your values credo? If yes, which ones?
7. Did you take an eclectic approach and use parts of all or several credos? If so, which ones?

Notes

1. James C. Collins and William C. Lazier, *Beyond Entrepreneurship: Turning Your Business into an Enduring Great Company* (Englewood Cliffs, N.J.: Prentice Hall, 1992), 66.
2. "Opening Session Features Ken Blanchard at Wooddale Church," *Compass* 3, no. 3 (February 1994): 1.
3. James C. Collins and Jerry I. Porras, *Built to Last* (New York: Harper Business, 1994), 219.

Part 2

The Mission of Your Ministry

4

The Definition of Mission

What Is a Mission?

It was 2:00 A.M. and Pastor Andy sat at the dining-room table engrossed in the book on ministry basics from his friend. It was a book that covered not only a ministry's core values but other concepts such as a ministry's mission. Several hours earlier his wife had tried to coax him to come to bed. Finally, she gave up and retired. As he paused to rest his eyes and reflect on what he was reading, Andy noted how quiet and peaceful it was at this time of the morning.

The book stated that few churches have formulated a concise, biblical mission statement that provides the direction for the ministry. The result is that many churches are like airplanes that have taken off but don't know where they're going. Some cautiously hover around the field while others bravely launch off in a particular direction only to become hopelessly lost. Lake Country resembled the former. They were hovering and going nowhere.

Pastor Andy had preached his heart out over the past year. The congregation had initially responded to his sermons. He was new and his style was so different from that of the former pastor. Not much happened as the result of his preaching, however, and he wanted to see results—lives changed. He had read somewhere that most people forget 95 percent of the sermon within seventy-two hours. His ministry was living proof of this maxim. Was this all there was to pastoral ministry?

The idea of a ministry mission excited him. It made much sense for several reasons. First, the church needed a clear, compelling ministry direction. A well-focused mission statement provides the destination on the map toward which the entire ministry takes flight. It can then focus all its energy in a single direction. Second, the church desperately needed to know what they were supposed to be doing. A mission statement helps the ministry to determine precisely its biblical function. It answers the question: What is the primary thing that God has called us to accomplish in this community? Third, the church needed to look to the future. The mission statement predetermines the ministry's future. We cannot predict the future; however, the formulation of a succinct mission statement will help to create a ministry's preferred future. The development of a ministry mission also provides boundaries for decision making, inspires ministry unity, encourages helpful change, and shapes the ministry's strategies.

The most important question for Pastor Andy at this early stage in his ministry is definitional and developmental: What is a mission and how do you develop one for your church? The next chapter will address mission development. This chapter will define mission by discussing briefly what it isn't and then what it is. It will close with an examination of the various kinds of missions.

What a Mission Is Not

People confuse a number of concepts with mission. In this section, I want to focus on the two most common concepts—vision and purpose.

A Mission Isn't a Vision

The concept of mission is older than that of vision. A brief survey of the books on management that you find on the shelves of most libraries reveals that the word *mission* has been in use in management circles for a number of years. When I wrote *Developing a Vision for Ministry in the Twenty-first Century*, few if anyone was using the word *vision*. I was aware of only one other book on the topic by Southern Baptist pastor Robert Dale that proved to be far ahead of its time. There are few books totally devoted to this topic even today. Many, however, refer to the concept in speech and in books relating to leadership and management.

As I travel and conduct seminars on leadership, I have come to expect the question: What is the difference between a vision and a mission? The words aren't synonyms as some leaders might think them to be. They have some elements in common but others that are different. This is such an important question that rather than briefly discuss it here, I have written chapter 7 to answer it. In chapter 7 I show that while the two concepts have at least four common characteristics, they differ from one another in at least eleven ways. For example, they are defined differently, applied differently, are different in length, purpose, and activity.

A Mission Isn't a Purpose

My studies reveal that most people equate mission and purpose. They argue that an organization's purpose is to accomplish its mission. I believe that they are different for Christian organizations in at least three ways. First, the mission asks the *what* question: What has God called this ministry to accomplish? The answer to this question is the organization's mission. The purpose, however, asks and answers an entirely different question. It answers the *why* question: Why has God placed you here? The answer is the organization's purpose. It is the reason why the ministry does what it does (its mission).

There is a second distinction—the mission serves as a target at which the ministry takes aim. In the case of the church, that target is the Great Commission (Matt. 28:19–20; Mark 16:15). The church's mission is to make disciples. The ministry organization's purpose, however, goes far beyond its target—it is the organization's reason for being. It is much more fundamental to the ministry. Whereas the church's mission is the Great Commission, its purpose is to glorify God (Ps. 22:23; 50:15; Isa. 24:15; Rom. 15:6; 1 Cor. 6:20; 10:31). The mission serves the purpose, but the mission is not the same as the purpose.

The third distinction further clarifies the second. Not only does the mission come under the umbrella of the purpose of the organization but so do a number of other ministry concepts. A ministry's core values—the topic of chapters 1 through 3—exist to glorify God. The same is true of the vision, strategy, and other vital ministry elements. Like the ministry mission, they, too, serve the purpose but are not the same as the purpose.

What a Mission Is

Often it helps to discover what something is by examining first what it isn't. Now that we have done this and have eliminated two confusing elements, it's time for a definition. I define a ministry mission as: a broad, brief, biblical statement of what the organization is supposed to be doing. This definition contains five essential elements.

A Mission Is Broad

The first defining element is breadth. It is essential that a ministry's mission be broad or all-embracing. The institution's master goal takes precedence over all its other goals. Mission is the umbrella over all the institution's ministry activities. This means that all the goals and activities should fit comfortably under the overarching ministry mission. If a goal or activity doesn't fit under the mission, then either the mission isn't broad enough or the goal or activity isn't within the scope of the mission and should be discontinued.

The following is the mission statement of Matthew Road Baptist Church located in Grand Prairie, Texas.

> Our mission is to share the love of God with the people of the mid-cities and beyond so that they can become fully devoted followers of Christ.

This mission is broad and includes all that Christ has commissioned the church to do. Essentially, the Great Commission divides into evangelism and edification. Everything a church can do would fit under one or the other. We find both in Matthew Road Baptist's mission statement. The church begins with sharing the love of God. That is evangelism. Its mission doesn't stop there, however. It moves new believers and established Christians toward maturity, toward being "fully devoted followers of Christ."

A mission needs breadth, but it should not be too broad. Too much breadth serves only to confuse followers and says very little. The following is a fictitious mission statement for an inner-city ministry.

> The mission of the Metroplex Foundation is to provide a "city of hope" for all its citizens where God is glorified.

This is too broad. It doesn't say anything. For example, what is a "city of hope?" I would assume that because it's a mission to the inner city it is trying to bring hope to people living in the inner city. But what does that mean? Is it hope as found in Christ? Is it leading people to faith in Christ, or does it only involve feeding people? This ministry statement is too vague to have any impact. In addition, the problem is compounded by including the phrase, "where God is glorified." What does that mean? I suspect that it means different things to different people. The important question is: What does it mean to the ministry organization? It isn't wrong to include a statement about glorifying Christ or God—that is very biblical. It would be much clearer, however, to replace it with a brief statement that says specifically how God is being glorified.

A Mission Is Brief

The second defining element of a mission statement is brevity. Brevity determines the size or length of a mission. No standard or fixed regulation for a mission statement exists, and a cursory examination of corporate mission statements reveals a variety of sizes or lengths. I argue that the mission statement should be short. Some say that it should be limited to fifteen or twenty pages in length. Others say that it should be one page or less. My response is that both are too long. Fifteen to twenty pages is excessive, and even one page is too much.

How short is brief? I believe that a good mission statement can and should be no more than a single sentence. My experience has been that the best mission statements are single, well-written sentences. A characteristic of highly effective organizations, no matter how complex, is that they can summarize what they're supposed to be doing in a succinct, simple way.

Randy Frazee, the senior pastor of Pantego Bible Church in Arlington, Texas, tells the following story of a meeting that his church administrator attended where Peter Drucker was the main speaker. A participant asked Drucker how long a mission statement should be. He responded, "If you can get the mission statement on a T-shirt, then it's probably the appropriate length."[1] Therefore, the critical test for a mission statement is whether it passes the T-shirt test; is it short enough to fit on a T-shirt?

Several churches have developed excellent mission statements that illustrate the value of a single-sentence mission statement. Willow Creek Community Church, located in Barrington, Illinois, developed this succinct statement:

> Our mission is to turn irreligious people into fully devoted followers of Christ.

In this case, Willow Creek could have used several pages to explain what the phrase, *fully devoted follower of Christ* is. No doubt some people would appreciate and gain from this knowledge; however, such length would have served only to bury most of their people in minutiae.

There are several reasons why good mission statements are brief. The first is communication. A key to clear, effective communication is brevity, not verbosity. People tend to read and pay more attention to short written statements, not to those of one or more pages. Second, short statements are more easily understood. More information may not clarify but only serve to confuse. Third, people remember succinct sentences. Once you add a second sentence or a third, congregants will abandon any attempt to memorize the mission.

A Mission Is Biblical

People have used the word *biblical* in a number of ways. One is that if a mission is biblical, it has to be found in the Bible. This means that every church and parachurch ministry must find their mission somewhere within Scripture. Those who develop the mission statement are to search through the Bible until they find a verse that gives them a mission. Then, that verse essentially becomes the mission. This view is quite restrictive. I prefer the view that the mission agrees with Scripture. While it doesn't necessarily have to be found in the pages of the Bible, it must not disagree with the teaching of Scripture.

A biblical mission is from God. He is the source of all missions. He may reveal your mission through the Bible or he may use some other means. Again, the mission must agree with, not contradict, the Bible. There are numerous mission statements that are sprinkled throughout the Old and New Testaments that are clearly from God. Let's briefly examine five in the Old Testament. The first belongs to Adam and Eve. God communicates their mission statement in Genesis 1:28: "God blessed them and said to them, 'Be fruitful and increase in number; fill the earth and subdue it. Rule over the fish of the sea and the birds of the air and over every living creature that moves on the ground.'" They were to have dominion over creation.

A second is Moses' mission. God revealed it to Moses in Exodus 3:10: "So now, go. I am sending you to Pharaoh to bring my people the Israelites out of Egypt." This one sentence sums up this leader's mission that extended over all that took place as recorded in Genesis through Deuteronomy.

A third is Joshua's mission. God presents it in Joshua 1:2: "Moses my servant is dead. Now then, you and all these people, get ready to cross the Jordan River into the land I am about to give them—to the Israelites." God's mission was to move Israel out of Egypt and into Canaan. He used two leaders with separate missions to accomplish his mission. Moses was to lead God's people out of bondage in Egypt. Joshua was to lead them into Canaan—the Promised Land.

A fourth is Isaiah's mission. In Isaiah 6:9 God commands the prophet: "Go and tell this people: 'Be ever hearing, but never understanding; be ever seeing, but never perceiving. Make the heart of this people callused; make their ears dull and close their eyes. Otherwise they might see with their eyes, hear with their ears, understand with their hearts, and turn and be healed." This must have been a frustrating mission for Isaiah. It was to result in little spiritual progress.

A fifth is Jeremiah's mission statement. The Lord communicates it in Jeremiah 1:10: "See, today I appoint you over nations and kingdoms to uproot and tear down, to destroy and overthrow, to build and to plant." In short, Jeremiah's mission was to proclaim to God's people a message of blessing and judgment.

There are several mission statements in the New Testament. One is the Savior's. His God-given mission is revealed in Mark 10:45: "For even the Son of Man did not come to be served, but to serve, and to give his life as a ransom for many." Jesus' mission was one of service. He would serve humankind to the point that he would pay the ultimate price—the sacrifice of his life for the sins of the world.

God has also given the church its mission. Matthew recorded it in Matthew 28:19–20: "Therefore go and make disciples of all nations. . . ." Mark recorded the same in Mark 16:15: "Go into all the world and preach the good news to all creation." It's the Great Commission mission that involves moving people from wherever they are in their relationship to God (lost or saved) to where God wants them to be (mature). The reason that the early church's mission is so important to us in the present is that its mission is our mission. The mission that Christ gave to the church in the first century is the same that he gives to us for the twenty-first century.

A Mission Is a Statement

A fourth defining element is that the mission is a statement. Every ministry must articulate its mission in some type of statement if its people are to know and understand their overall goal. This is a major problem for many churches across North America. Most haven't articulated a mission statement. Most likely, this is because they don't have one.

A mission statement may be verbal or written; however, I believe that leaders best communicate their visions with verbal statements and their missions with written statements. When people see the mission statement on paper, they know in their heads where the ministry is going. Writing out the mission in the form of a statement forces you to gather your thoughts and clearly think through what you're saying. When a leader can clearly write his or her mission on paper, then most likely it is a well-thought-through statement.

Writing out the mission statement puts it in a form that you can communicate in a variety of ways. One is to place it prominently on the church's bulletin, brochure, or newsletter where all can see it and be regularly reminded of it. Another is to include it in a statement that is read and discussed in a newcomers or new member's class, which is imperative because new members and interested people must obtain ownership of the mission in order to be involved with the ministry. The mission could be framed or put on a wall plaque and hung in a church's foyer or its main offices. You could place it on wallet-size cards for the people who are a part of the ministry to keep with them, or follow Peter Drucker's advice and actually put it on a T-shirt. Then people could wear it around the house as well as around the ministry. It would serve as a constant reminder of the ministry's mission.

A Mission Is What the Ministry Is Supposed to Do

A fifth defining element is that a mission is what the ministry is supposed to accomplish. It's your ministry's primary goal or task. It's what "business" you're in. It's not what you want to do, but what God wants you to do. The vital mission question is: What is this ministry supposed to do? This appears to be such a simple question, yet too few ministry organizations are asking it. A major reason for the decline of so many churches that were vibrant in the 1940s and 1950s is that they have forgotten their mission or what business they are in. Most if not all began with a leader who had a clear mission for the church. That mission had much to do with why the church was planted. With the passing of time and a relative degree of success, however, that mission has been lost and left behind while the institution moves forward.

A key to revitalizing many of these churches and similar ministries is too ask the mission question. Peter Drucker writes: "We are mission-focused. What are we trying to do? Don't ever forget that first question. The mission must come first. This is the lesson of the last fifty to one hundred years. The moment we lose sight of the mission we are gone."[2] The same is true for church planting. A new church must begin with a clear mission that is strategically positioned in such a way that no one forgets it with the passing of time.

The mission question, What is our ministry supposed to do? is directional and diagnostic. It is directional for new ministries whether church or parachurch. When they answer this question, they know where they are supposed to be going and what they are supposed to be doing.

The mission question is diagnostic for older, established ministries. It is the first of five questions, The Ministry Mission Audit, that will help a ministry diagnose its state of existence. The answer to the first question, What does God want us to do? takes the ministry to the Bible. Do the Scriptures directly or indirectly answer this question? We saw above that the church's mission is the Great Commission: pursuing lost people, reaching lost people, and then discipling them (Matt. 20:19–20). So, the first diagnostic question is: Are we pursuing and winning lost people and then helping them mature in the faith? They are responsible to grow, but the church is responsible to put in place a strategy to help them grow.

The second diagnostic question is: What are we doing? While Christ has commissioned the church to make disciples, far too many aren't accomplishing this task today. Some function much as a convalescent home. They have people who are saying, "Look, I've done my part, now it's time for somebody else to take care of me." The problem is that there are fewer young people around to take care of them. Others function as safe cognitive communities. They are one big happy (and in some cases not-so-happy) Bible study group. They know much about the Bible but not many people outside the community come to faith. Others are evangelistic centers where people come to faith in Christ but fall into nominal Christianity because there is no program to take them any further in Christlikeness.

The third diagnostic question assumes that there is a discrepancy between questions one and two. It asks: Why aren't we doing what God want us to be doing? When you ask this question in a church board meeting, people quickly become uncomfortable. They shift their bodies around and clear their throats, and the room becomes strangely quiet. There exists a variety of answers. The most common is that today's typical church has become inward focused. They are simply trying to take care of their current congregations and to keep the doors open. Another is that the pastor is strong in an area such as preaching but not in evangelism. Other answers are disobedience, fatigue, hidden agendas, ignorance, and so on.

The fourth question forces people to look to the institution's future without a biblical mission. It asks: If we continue on our present course, where will we be two, five, or ten years from now? The answer for a growing church is that it levels off. The answer for a leveled off church is that it declines. And the answer for a declining church is that it no longer exists.

The fifth question focuses on the leadership. It asks: Do our key leaders know where the ministry is and where it's going? It also asks: Do they agree on that direction? My experience with some older, traditional churches that are struggling is that they are ignoring the present and the future while looking to and wishing for a return to the past.

The sixth question assumes that the ministry is merely circling the airport or is flying off course. It asks: What will it take to change course and move in a God-ordained direction? The answer is critical. A good answer is: Whatever it takes—as long as it doesn't contradict Scripture. But this is difficult for ministries which have been pursuing other missions for years. Another answer is: A miracle. Most often, this is the answer of a dying ministry. There is not much hope here.

The final question is: Are you and the leadership willing to do whatever it takes to move the ministry in a new direction? Essentially, this is an obedience issue. The call is for repentance and response to God's clear directive in his Word. It's much easier to talk about than to accomplish. Failure to act places the entire ministry in jeopardy, and long-term disobedience may result in the death of the institution as happened to the churches in Revelation 2 and 3.

The Ministry Mission Audit

1. According to Scripture, what does God want you to do?
2. What are you doing?
3. If there's a discrepancy, why aren't you doing what God wants you to do?
4. If you continue on your present course, where will the ministry be two, five, or ten years from now?

5. Do your key leaders know where the ministry is and where it's going?
6. What will it take to change course and move in a new direction?
7. Are you and the leadership willing to do whatever it takes to move the ministry in a new direction?

The Kinds of Missions

We can further enhance our understanding of the mission by investigating the personal mission, the organizational mission, and the departmental mission.

The Personal Mission

So far we have talked about organizational mission. That is because it's the topic of this book. Your organizational mission, however, is not the priority. Your personal mission is. What your organizational mission is to your ministry, your personal mission is to your life. Therefore, the development of your personal mission should precede that of your organizational mission. Your personal mission determines what you will do with your life and how you'll serve Christ. This, in turn, may lead to your service in a particular ministry organization. Once you have determined this and have aligned with that organization, you are ready to develop a mission for that organization.

I encourage you to develop a personal mission statement before you develop your organizational mission statement. Here are some questions whose answers will help you determine your mission in life. (1) What do you want to do with your life? (2) What does God want you to do with your life? (3) If God gave you one wish for your life, what would it be? (4) What legacy do you want to leave behind? (5) How do you want others, your friends and family, to remember you after you're gone?

If you are in your twenties or thirties, you may struggle with these questions. The reason is that you may not have had much experience in life or ministry, so you're unsure of your answers. Should this be your situation, I encourage you to pursue the discovery of your divine design. It consists of your natural and spiritual gifts, your talents and abilities, your passion (what you feel strongly about), your temperament, and many other things.

Writing a personal mission statement helps you to determine what God wants you to do with your life. That is most important. It also assists you in making good decisions about matters that affect your life. For example, some organizations may offer you a position with them. Now you have to make a decision: Do I go with them and move on, or do I stay where I am? You evaluate your options and make a decision based on your mission statement. These decisions will serve to refine your mission statement because they will teach you much about yourself. A personal mission statement can make the difference between mediocre service for Christ and exceptional service. Writing for the marketplace, Michael Gerber says, "I believe it's true that the difference between great people and everyone else is that great people create their lives actively, while everyone else is created by their lives, passively waiting to see where life takes them next."[3] Gerber's words remind me of Paul's in 1 Corinthians 9:24, "Do you not know that in a race all the runners run, but only one gets the prize? Run in such a way as to get the prize."

The Organizational Mission

Once you have determined your personal mission in life, then you are ready to develop an organizational mission. I use the word *organizational*. Other words that also apply are *congregational*, *institutional*, and *corporate*. The organizational mission should be in line with your personal mission. For example, God may have designed you to lead a church as its pastor. Therefore, you as the pastor of the church should develop its organizational mission by implementing the Great Commission through the local church ministry. It would be a mistake for you to pursue some other career such as selling insurance or servicing computers.

The Departmental Mission

The departmental mission is under the umbrella of the organization's mission. As a church or parachurch ministry grows in size, it will organize itself into different departments. For example, a church might have departments responsible for worship, Christian education, evangelism, and so on. Each of these departments should develop its own mission statement to show how it contributes to the overall, or master, mission of the ministry.

The departmental mission has three benefits. First, it brings the mission concept down to the grassroots level. It emphasizes and serves as a constant reminder of the importance of mission and what the organization as well as the department is all about. Second, it shows how each department contributes to the whole. This demonstrates the importance of each department in accomplishing the overall mission of the organization. It announces to all that everyone is an important part of the institution and that everyone has a vital stake in it. Finally, it serves to keep each department focused not only on what the institution is supposed to be doing but also on what each department is supposed to be doing. This discourages either from moving off in its own direction.

Not long ago I visited and toured Willow Creek Community Church. As I walked by the various departments within the church, I noticed that they had mounted each department's mission statement on a prominent wall in each area.

Dallas Seminary is a parachurch organization that has an institutional mission. Since it's one of the larger seminaries, it consists of a number of departments such as Christian education, languages, field education, human resources, and so on. One department is the physical plant that is responsible for maintaining the facilities that are vital to the school's operation. The physical plant has developed the following mission statement:

> The mission of the physical plant is to serve the Dallas Theological Seminary community with a professional and personable attitude by providing a physical environment that is conducive to the DTS mission of preparing godly servant-leaders in the body of Christ worldwide.

Questions for Thought and Discussion

1. Do you have a personal mission statement? Are you convinced of the importance of such a statement? Why or why not? How might a personal mission statement make a difference in your life?
2. Does your ministry organization have a mission statement? If yes, what is it? Is it a good one? If the organization doesn't, then why not?
3. What is your ministry supposed to be doing? What is it actually doing? Are your answers to these two questions the same or is there a discrepancy between them? If there's a discrepancy, how do you explain it?
4. If your ministry continues on its present course, where do you envision it in two years? In five years? In ten years?
5. Does the primary leader of the ministry and the board know where the ministry is presently and where it's going? Why or why not?
6. What will it take for your ministry to change and do what it's supposed to do? Is the leadership (president, pastor, board) willing to change? Why or why not? Are the people willing to change? Explain.

Notes

1. Randy Frazee with Lyle E. Schaller, *The Comeback Congregation* (Nashville: Abingdon, 1995), 6.
2. Peter Drucker, "The New Models," *NEXT* 1, no. 2 (August 1995): 2.
3. Michael Gerber, *The E-Myth* (New York: Harper Business, 1986), 85.

5

The Development of a Mission
How to Make Your Mission

Pastor Andy purchased a copy of the book on ministry basics for all his board members. Their practice over the years had been to buy and read a book on some topic that they felt might help them improve as leaders, so at Andy's urging, they had agreed to read and discuss this book together. There developed some uneasiness in their meetings because the material was so foreign to what they were doing in the church. This uneasiness came to a head when they all took the ministry mission audit.

All the members worked on the first question at home but came together to discuss their answers. There was some initial disagreement over what they felt the church was supposed to do. Some where not well grounded in the Scriptures and held divergent opinions that they voiced rather strongly; however, as they studied Christ's proclamation of the Great Commission in Matthew 28:19–20, Mark 16:15, and Acts 1:8, the Scriptures had a penetrating effect (Heb. 4:12) and most of them eventually agreed that they were in the disciple-making business.

The second question sobered a number of the members. When they compared what they were supposed to be doing with what they were doing, they discovered a major contradiction. One influential, elderly board member commented, "We haven't seen someone come to faith in Christ in years. Wouldn't it be great to see people accept Christ as they did back in the good old days when the church was on fire?" At this point, Andy chimed in, "This book points out that a well-thought-out, biblical mission statement would help immensely in realizing the kind of evangelism that took place in the early days of this church." With this, the entire room was silent. But it was a positive silence. Andy could see that the men were quietly excited as they thought about the evening's discussion.

Then, of all people, Harry Smith raised his hand and tentatively asked, "How would we go about developing a mission for our church?" Andy was shocked. Harry was the one you could always count on to slam the brakes on any kind of change. Andy saw his chance, so he quickly responded, "The next chapter explains how to develop a mission statement. Why don't we give it a shot? Let's work on one and see what we come up with." The moment was right, and the men responded positively.

Harry Smith's question is most important to any ministry. How do you develop a coherent, biblical mission statement? The answer is the three *p* words: *personnel*, *preparation*, and *process*. I have designed this chapter to help you work your way through the three *p*s as you develop a mission statement for your ministry.

The Mission Development Personnel

It's imperative that farmers farm. If others such as those who finance the farmer or those who sell him his equipment should attempt to replace the farmer, the results would be disastrous. The first *p* stands for the ministry personnel who make up the mission-development team. The right people must be involved in the process. The questions are: Who are the right people? Who should develop the mission statement?

I advise most church and parachurch ministries to try the following. The pastor or lead person initiates and develops a mission. This is an essential act of leadership that involves placing an initial document on the table. Then, other vital people who are on the leadership team are invited to review and evaluate it. My experience is that it's most difficult to ask a group of people to design a mission statement from nothing; thus this approach gives them an idea of what it is you're attempting to do and something to react to as well. It allows them to get their fingerprints all over the statement and experience a sense of ownership.

The most effective mission statements reflect the hearts of their people. A mission has to be something that both the leadership and the people can share. Peter Drucker points out that it's your people who determine the performance capacity of your organization. More importantly, the New Testament teaches the same principle (Ephesians 4; 1 Corinthians 12; and Romans 12). If your people don't feel some ownership, then they aren't likely to commit to the mission. It then becomes your mission, not their mission.

How many people should you involve? The general principle is that too many cooks spoil the broth. In chapters 2 and 3 we learned that the size of the ministry directly affects those who are involved. If the ministry is a small church, it can include some of its members as well as its leaders (see figure 2.1), which elicits more input from those at the grassroots level. You find out what is on the hearts of the men and women in the pews. The downside is that this method allows the church's squeaky wheels (those who resist change) to express their opinions.

A larger ministry will not be able to involve many people at the grassroots level due to its sheer size. These ministries will depend on the senior pastor, the staff, the board, other key leaders, and small group leaders who represent the various segments of the congregation. These people are to give input and help develop the ministry mission. Some churches would be wise to conduct "town hall" meetings at which the senior pastor and staff present the mission and elicit responses from the congregation at large. You should keep in mind, however, that too much input from too many people will only serve to neuter a good mission statement. Finally, whether a large or small church, it is wise to have the congregation vote on the mission statement because it affects the direction of the entire church.

I also suggest that you consider the use of a consultant in developing your mission as well as your core values, vision, and other key concepts. It's important that you do the ministry nuts and bolts well. A qualified, skilled consultant brings much knowledge and expertise to the process, including fresh objectivity. He or she will save you time, and the quality of the product will more than offset expenses.

The Mission Development Preparation

The temptation for many leaders is to move too quickly. They want to jump immediately into the mission-development process. However, preparation must precede process. The seasoned farmer knows that before he plants his crops, he must prepare the soil or an anemic harvest will be the result. The mission-development process also requires the preparation of the ministry soil if it is to produce a healthy fruitful mission statement. The preparation stage consists of answering five critical questions.

Is There a Need for a Ministry Mission?

The answer to this question at this point seems obvious and perhaps even silly. However, it isn't so obvious or silly to the board member who hasn't read about these basic ministry concepts and is reeling in the wake of all the change that is crashing in around him as he moves into the twenty-first century. Many have assumed a defensive posture, hoping that all the turbulence will blow over and that life will return to normal very soon.

The answer is not as obvious to those who are currently in a successful ministry either. Why develop a mission statement when everything is going well? As the old-timer once quipped, "If it ain't broke, why fix it?" My point is that if those responsible for developing a ministry mission don't see the need, then you're wasting your time. In some situations, you could cause your ministry harm by pursuing such a venture. People resist and even resent doing that for which they don't feel a sense of need.

Regardless of where people are regarding the need, you would be wise to take time to prepare the soil for the mission seed. The best way to accomplish this is to follow the lead of Pastor Andy and take the ministry mission audit presented in the previous chapter. The lead person in a parachurch ministry and the pastor of a church should take it first. Then they should lead their boards and relevant personnel through the process as well.

Is the Ministry Ready for a Mission?

If the ministry sees a need for developing a mission, then the ministry would seem to be ready for a mission. Even if the need is realized, however, a ministry may not be ready to proceed because of busyness, for example. A church leader may be so busy trying to keep the church afloat and still do the work of the ministry that he or she believes there is not enough time to develop a mission. It becomes just one more burdensome item on the ministry to-do list. What the leader doesn't realize is that a dynamic mission statement has the potential to mobilize some of the inactive people so that they become more involved in the ministry and thus take some of the load off him or her.

Another reason against proceeding is hopelessness. The ministry is dying and is at a point of no return. Those few stalwarts who have stayed with the ministry feel that to invest further effort in trying to keep the ministry alive is futile. It would be akin to investing in a business that is on its last leg. However, a dynamic mission statement has the potential to breathe life-giving oxygen into a dying ministry and revive it.

How Much Time Will It Take to Develop a Mission?

There's a popular maxim that says: If anything is worth doing, then it's worth doing well. The question is, How much time should you set aside if you want to develop an excellent mission statement? While it will take some quality time if it's to be done well, it will not take as much time as some of the other ministry ABCs such as the core values, the vision, and the strategy.

It's conceivable that a team of leaders could develop a well-prepared mission statement in three to five sessions that last several hours each with some reflective time in between. Much depends on how well the team works together. My experience is that most team problems are either philosophical or relational, not theological. If there is initial agreement on their core values, vision, and other key areas of culture, the development session will go much faster. When I conduct mission-development sessions with unified boards, we average from one to two hours, providing they agree on their core values. This is another reason why I advise ministries to develop their core values before their mission statements.

Preparation is important because the more that team members know about mission development going into the process the better. A book like this one can prove helpful and save much time in preparing the soil. Also, it is difficult to create an original mission statement. You may want to provide the team with a number of sample mission statements that will prod their thinking. You might benefit by using some of those provided later in this chapter.

Where Is the Best Place to Develop a Mission?

Because developing a mission statement takes less time than some of the other basics, you may want to use your own facilities, such as the church building instead of going to a retreat setting. This affords several advantages. One is that you don't have to sleep in a strange place, which is problematic for some who find it difficult to sleep in a place that they aren't accustomed to. A second is that you don't have to spend any time away from your family. A third is that you have all the equipment you need with you. Invariably, when a team takes a planned retreat, they leave some important item behind. Finally, you don't waste any time traveling. However, using your own facilities has its disadvantages, such as interruptions and distractions. You aren't very far from the telephone or individuals who believe that their problems are major emergencies that must be dealt with immediately.

Some people prefer to get away from home. Often a different environment can spark the creative processes more than a familiar one. People like to retreat to a mountain home or a nearby lake. They find that this allows more time for intense, creative reflection. They are able to focus more on the problems and issues at hand when they are away. Also, they are better able to enjoy one another's company.

If you decide on a retreat setting, the distance can be long or short. I went on a retreat with a board from a church in Dallas, Texas. We traveled to Bransom, Missouri, where we held our meetings in a motel located on a mountain lake. One of the elders flew us there in his own plane, and we were gone for only a day. One of the departments at Dallas Seminary chose to retreat to a health facility only a block away that provides rooms for meetings. When the day was over, the team had the option to swim, sit in the sauna, jog, or use the workout equipment before going home. My home church opted to retreat to a western ranch about twenty miles out of town. The ranch had special facilities for group meetings. At the end of the day, the staff finished their time together with a sumptuous steak supper.

How Much Will It Cost to Develop a Mission?

Most professional people value their time more than their money. Thus, this question is important. Actually, your answer to the previous question affects your answer to this question. If you use your own facilities, the cost will be minimal. You might choose to take the team out for a hearty lunch or a steak supper. Some local institutions such as banks have meeting rooms that they allow others to use as a courtesy.

If you travel to some off-site location, the cost will be greater. You will need to budget for travel expenses such as gasoline and wear and tear on automobiles. You will also need to allow for the rental of several rooms, refreshments, and meals.

The bottom line is to answer the question: How much is it worth to your ministry to have the best mission statement possible? The answer is that it could make the difference between the success and failure of the ministry institution.

The Mission Development Process

Once you know who is going to develop the ministry mission (the mission personnel) and you have prepared the soil (the mission preparation), the third *p* is the mission process. What is that process? What are the steps that you and your team should take to develop the mission product? You'll find the answer in the definition of the mission. In chapter 4 I defined a ministry mission as a broad, brief, biblical statement of what your organization is supposed to be doing. This definition is key to the mission development process. If you can remember the definition, you can also remember the process.

The way to develop your mission is to use each of the key elements in the definition as a step in the process. The rest of this chapter will examine these as we walk through the process. For your working convenience, I have included a summary of this process in appendix E.

Determine What You're Supposed to Be Doing According to the Scriptures

Step one begins with the last element in the definition, that it is a statement of what your organization is supposed to be doing. It combines with the third that says it should be biblical. The direct or indirect source of your mission is the Bible. What does the Bible say that your church or parachurch ministry should be doing? Answering this question means that God determines your mission. Three miniquestions will aid you with step one.

Are you involved in a church or parachurch ministry? You may categorize a Christian ministry as either church or parachurch. If you serve Christ in a church, then he has already predetermined your ministry mission. It's the Great Commission as found in Matthew 28:19–20 and Mark 16:15. Christ has commissioned your church to make disciples.

You may also serve the Savior in a parachurch context. The Bible will address your mission directly or indirectly. Whatever your ministry, you should begin the mission-developing process by searching the Scriptures to determine what they say about what you want to accomplish as a ministry. If your ministry focuses on evangelism, what does the Bible say about evangelism?

Whom are you attempting to serve? A ministry must focus on people, not programs. This is because ministry is people centered not program centered. Since you can't reach everybody, you must ask, Who will I reach (your future ministry constituency) and, Who am I reaching (present ministry constituency)? Both questions are essential. If your present or future ministry consists of older people, then you'll probably attract older people. If it consists of younger people, then it will attract other young people. In the latter part of the twentieth century, the majority of churches have targeted Christians and virtually ignored non-Christians. However, many new churches at the turn of the century are not only ministering to their present constituency (members), but are targeting seekers—those who are lost but interested in spiritual matters.

Most would answer the above question as to who they are trying to reach with, "our community." While that in some cases is a valid answer, many who attend the church may not live in its community. The parish system in North America is dead. Consequently, another answer might be, "unchurched people." To target churched people is to steal sheep. Should you practice this, you and your church will be very unpopular with other churches in the area. Instead, why not target unchurched people both lost and saved outside your community as well as in it.

How will you minister to people? The final question gets at the nature of your ministry to people. It asks: What are you going to do for people? What services will you provide for them? Will you attempt to win people to Christ and lead Christians to a deeper walk with Christ? If you are a church, then you are to attempt an even balance between the two. Parachurch ministries have an easier time knowing how they will minister to people because they begin with a specific ministry service in mind such as evangelism, discipleship, stewardship, and others.

What does a good mission statement look like? The following example for a fictitious church answers well the above questions.

The mission of Grace Church is to lead the people of southern Collin County to faith in Christ and growth in Christlikeness.

Answering the first question of determining what you're supposed to be doing according to the Scriptures will always be easy. This is obviously a church ministry because its mission is the Great Commission. It clearly designates whom it will serve—the people of southern Collin County. It also clarifies how it will serve them—it will lead them to faith in Christ and growth in Christlikeness.

Articulate Your Mission in a Written Statement

The next step in developing your mission is to get it down on paper. According to my definition, a mission is a statement of what your ministry is supposed to be doing. The power of the mission statement is that it's written, not spoken. Writing the mission statement blows the cobwebs off the brain. It forces you to clarify and focus your thinking about your mission. If you know it, you can write it down. There are several miniquestions that will help you to take this second step.

What words communicate best with your people? It takes some time to write a good mission statement. The mission drafters will need to shape and reshape, draft and redraft the statement until it's just right. Much of this involves its wording. This involves personalizing the mission. You want to choose the words that best fit your people and to some degree your target audience. (The mission statement is primarily for your people.) For example, old familiar clichés turn off a younger audience, whereas, fresh contemporary terms attract them.

A demographic study of your present or target audience will provide you with the information you need to make these determinations. A demographic study equips you with information such as people's education, marital status, employment, number of children, and so on. If you are presently in a ministry, then much of this information will be at your fingertips. I've noticed, however, that a number of ministries tend to ignore demographic studies to their disadvantage; thus they lose touch with their people. If you are starting a new ministry, there are a number of professional organizations that will provide this kind of information.[1] You may also wish to conduct your own congregational and community surveys.

You should also be aware of terms that are regional and limited to a particular part of the country. It's not wrong to use these terms. The warning is to make sure that your terms fit the region. Terms that make sense in Dallas, Texas, a distinct part of the South, might not make sense in New England. The following is a mission statement developed by Pastor Ken Carozza for Colonial Chapel in Connecticut.

Colonial Chapel exists to colonize Connecticut and the greater commonwealth with citizens of Heaven who possess a new spiritual constitution, who passionately embrace the revolutionary teachings of Jesus Christ, who have declared themselves "in dependence" upon God, His word and His people, and whose mission is to proclaim the truth which sets men free, liberating them from the rule of darkness.

Pastor Carozza has spent time carefully crafting and redrafting this statement to find the precise words for his ministry constituency. He uses words such as *commonwealth*, *constitution*, and *revolutionary* that are commonplace in New England but might seem out of place in some other region of the country.

Do your people understand what you've written? This raises the issue of clarity. If people don't understand your mission statement, then you don't have one! Christian ministries tend to use biblical terms in their mission statements. The problem is that, according to a Gallop poll, most Americans are biblically illiterate, and this has proved true in churches as well.

One popular word that has caused some clarity problems is *disciple*. It has proved problematic not only for the public in general but also for the Christian community in particular. The question is: What is a disciple? Consequently, some churches have used words that define the word *disciple* for their audience. One example is the mission statement of Willow Creek Community Church:

> The mission of Willow Creek Community Church is to turn irreligious people into fully devoted followers of Jesus Christ.

Willow Creek could have said that they desire to turn irreligious people into disciples. But what does that mean for their people—many of whom are former seekers who are just learning about their new faith? So Willow Creek opted for "fully devoted followers of Christ."

Another example is the mission statement of the church I pastor, Northwood Community Church in Dallas, Texas.

> Our mission is to develop people into fully functioning followers of Christ.

We also wrestled with the problematic word *disciple*. Our solution was to substitute the words "fully developing followers of Christ." To the casual reader or leader this may sound trivial; however, it could make the difference in people's understanding and implementing your ministry's mission. At Northwood, we define a fully functioning follower as one who is characterized by the three *c*s: conversion, commitment, and contribution.

A fully functioning follower has been converted to Christ, has committed his or her life to Christ, and is contributing to the cause of Christ.

Does your mission format convey your mission statement well? Your mission statement may take any one of a number of forms. The only limitation might be your creative abilities. I have discovered three formats that characterize most of the mission statements in my collection.

Format #1

The mission of (name of the ministry) is to _____

_____

An example is the statement of the fictional Crossroads Church of Oklahoma City, Oklahoma:

The mission of Crossroads Church is to win the lost and empower believers to become fully functioning followers of Christ.

This format is simple and gets to the point. Its disadvantage, however, is that it's formal and lacks a personal touch.

Format #2

Name of Your Ministry
Our mission is to _____

If Crossroads Church had adopted this format, it would look like the following:

Crossroads Church
Our mission is to win the lost and empower believers to become fully functioning followers of Christ.

This format has all the advantages of the first—it's simple and straightforward. The use of the personal pronoun "our" adds a personal touch.

Format #3

(Name of your ministry) seeks to _____

_____

Had Crossroads Church chosen this format, it would look like this:

Crossroads Church seeks to win the lost and empower believers to become fully functioning followers of Christ.

This format has all the advantages of the first. If you don't like the word *seeks*, you might choose to use some other verb such as *desires*, *aspires*, *aims*, *strives*, or exists. Format #3 also has some potential disadvantages. One is that it seems a little formal as does format #1. The second is that you might not know that it's a mission statement because it doesn't tell you what it is.

You have already noted that each format follows its verb with an infinitive. In the above example from Crossroads Church, the verb *seeks* is followed by the infinitive *to win* and the implied infinitive *to empower*. Choose the exact infinitive very carefully—not just any infinitive will do. The key is what you hope to accomplish for your target audience. You have already determined this in your answer to the third miniquestion of step 1. Chart 5.1 lists some infinitives that might prove helpful:

To assist	To develop	To establish	To produce
To create	To empower	To help	To promote
To craft	To energize	To lead	To provide
To convert	To equip	To prepare	To share

Chart 5.1: Helpful Infinitives

Strike a Balance Between Breadth and Clarity

Step 3 asks you to find the balance between breadth and clarity. They might appear to be opposites—the broader the statement, the less clear it is. The two, however, can coexist in dynamic tension. You want the mission statement to be both broad and clear at the same time. The temptation for most mission developers is to err to one extreme or the other. Your job is to land in between. Two miniquestions will help you do this.

Is your mission statement broad enough? The first element in the definition of a mission is breadth. Since most ministries conduct multiple functions, such as Christian education, small groups, worship, evangelism, and others, your statement should be broad enough to include all that you're doing in your ministry. Also, if a ministry function doesn't fit under your mission statement, either the statement isn't broad enough or the ministry function goes beyond the scope of your mission and you should jettison it. For example, a number of churches have decided to start Christian schools and some have planted Christian colleges. The question is: Is a Christian school a part of our mission statement? Does it fall under the mission umbrella? If not, then don't start one.

Is your mission statement clear? The danger with the first miniquestion is that a statement can become so broad that it doesn't say anything. As you work through the process, ask yourself and others: What specifically does this mean?

There are some words that mask ministry clarity. For example, some ministries will use the word *glory* as in "the glory of God" or "the glory of Christ." It appears in a statement that says the church desires to glorify God in some way. How can anyone object to such a term since it's biblical? The problem is: What does it mean specifically? Instead, use a different word such as honor and then go on to explain how, specifically, you will honor or glorify God. Wooddale Church has done this in their mission statement.

> The purpose of Wooddale Church is to honor God by making more disciples for Jesus Christ.

Another way to ensure mission clarity is to include a separate statement that provides further clarification, even though this could be awkward and burdensome.

A test of mission clarity is the "people test." The mission statement is primarily an in-house document. It is written for your people and for those outside the ministry who might be interested in becoming a part of the ministry. (It's not for the lost people whom you're attempting to reach with the Gospel.) Therefore, you should quiz your people. Ask them what the mission draft communicates to them. When it passes the people test, then you have achieved mission clarity.

Keep It Brief and Simple

Step four focuses on brevity that leads to simplicity. Brevity walks hand in hand with simplicity. The second element in my definition of a fully functional mission is that it is brief. The following four miniquestions will help you to accomplish this end.

Have you committed information overload? A characteristic of some who develop a mission is that they attempt to include too much in the statement. To achieve clarity, they want to pack as much information as possible into the product. Actually, this serves only to confuse those who need to understand and carry out the ministry's mission. People can handle only so much information. Consequently, we must include less, not more in our statements. Information overload is the enemy, not the friend of clarity.

I have observed that information overload masks itself in three basic forms. The first is to include a definition or explanation of the ministry in the mission statement. The following is a fictitious example:

> The mission of Hartford Divinity School as a professional, graduate-level school is to train future ministers to lead our denomination of churches.

The statement, "as a professional, graduate-level school," is a definition or explanation. It defines or explains who the Hartford Divinity School is. While this is important, it need not be in the mission statement. It qualifies as information overload. If the statement is in the school's catalog, then it's probably understood and not necessary. Otherwise, it might appear in a separate statement. Dropping the definition makes it more simple: The mission of Hartford Divinity School is to train future ministers to lead our denomination of churches.

A second form of overload is to include the strategy for accomplishing your mission or parts of your mission in the mission statement. This is the most common form of information overload that I have come across in working with churches. The following is an invented example:

> The mission of Grace Bible Church is to lead our people to growth in Christlikeness by equipping them through the exposition of God's word for ministry in the twenty-first century.

The entire statement, "by equipping them through the exposition of God's word for ministry in the twenty-first century" is strategy. It explains not what but how. It is important that people know how you plan to accomplish your mission. In fact, it's so important that it should appear in a strategy statement separate from the mission statement. To include it with the mission makes the latter needlessly complex. Phrases introduced by prepositions such as *by* and *through* are red flags that signal complexity when they are tacked onto the mission statement.

A third form of information overload is to include both a definition and the strategy in the same statement with the mission. This is the worst and most confusing form of overload:

> The mission of Hartford Divinity School as a professional, graduate-level school is to train future ministers to lead our denomination of churches by blending sociological studies and modern theological principles with training in ministry skills.

As before, the explanation or definition comes after the name of the school and is signaled by the word *as*. The prepositions *by* and *with* come at the end of the statement and signal strategy. The mission would be much simpler if these were dropped, revealing the mission statement itself: The mission of Hartford Divinity School is to train future ministers to lead our denomination of churches.

Does your statement pass the T-shirt test? The power of the mission statement is in its brevity and simplicity. Peter Drucker is correct when he says that a good mission statement should be short enough to fit on a T-shirt. It would be difficult to place the inflated, overloaded mission statement for Hartford Divinity School on a T-shirt. Even if you could, the letters would have to be so small that you might have difficulty reading it. The statement from Willow Creek, "our mission is to turn irreligious people into fully devoted followers of Christ," would fit on any T-shirt. The same is true of Pantego Bible Church's mission: "To transform people, through the work of the Holy Spirit, into fully developing followers of Christ."

Can you express your mission in one sentence? The best, most powerful mission statements are simple, one-sentence statements. They get right to the point. Note the power of each of the following mission sentences:

> Our mission is to transform people, through the work of the Holy Spirit, into fully developing followers of Christ.
> —Pantego Bible Church

> Our mission is to attack the enemy and defeat him.
> —United States Marine Corps

> Our mission is to make citizens out of the rejected.
> —The Salvation Army

> Our mission is to prepare men and women for ministry in the local churches.
> —Winebrenner Theological Seminary

Is your mission easily remembered? Our goal as leaders is to provide our people with a mission statement that is both easily understood and remembered. It should have staying power; it should stick to the ribs of one's mind. You don't want your people to attempt to memorize it. You want people to hear it several times and remember it naturally. This won't happen if you try to cram too much information into the statement or include an explanation of your ministry or your strategy. People simply won't put forth the mental effort that it takes to remember it. A case in point is the four one-sentence mission statements above. A few moments have elapsed since you read them. Can you remember any of them? Chances are excellent that if you read over them several times, even though there are four, you would remember them due to their succinctness and power.

Questions for Thought and Discussion

1. Who will write your mission statement? Why? Is this person responsible for initiating and completing the process? How many other people will be involved in this project? Who are they? Will you enlist the help of a consultant?

2. Are you and the other leaders in your ministry convinced that you need a clear, biblical mission? Why or why not? Have they taken the ministry mission audit? If yes, what did you learn from the audit?

3. Is the ministry ready to develop a mission? If yes, how do you know? If no, is it for the reasons mentioned in this chapter (busyness, hopelessness)? If not, then why?

4. How much time will it take for you to develop your mission statement? Do you anticipate any delays or interruptions? If so, what are they? Have you allowed for and encouraged some reflective time between meetings?

5. Where will you meet and why? Is it the best site for your team? How much will it cost? Is cost a big factor in your decision?

6. Work through the mission-development process as summarized in appendix E. What is your mission? Are you happy with it? Explain. Are the others happy with it? Why or why not? Does it need some more work?

7. Do you already have a mission statement? What is it? Use the mission-development process as a test of its quality. Is it a good one or does it need some more work?

Notes

1. See chapter 4 in my book, *Developing a Vision for Ministry in the Twenty-first Century* (Grand Rapids: Baker, 1992).

Part 3

The Vision of Your Ministry

6

The Definition of Vision - Part 1

What Is a Vision?

Pastor Andy spearheaded the mission-development process for his board. He correctly surmised mission development to be a necessary function of leadership on his part. He led the board through the mission-development process (see appendix E). They set aside a Saturday to work on it. Most viewed their Saturdays as a necessary day to catch up on household chores or to spend some badly needed time with their families; however, all felt that this was important enough to the church that they would gladly give up one Saturday. By 3:00 P.M. they had finished the process. Though mentally fatigued, Andy could tell that they were proud of what they had accomplished and were very much behind the new mission. It was theirs. It had their fingerprints all over it. They felt a powerful sense of ownership. As they left the meeting, they were smiling, shaking hands, and some even slapped Andy on the back.

Pastor Andy was delighted with their response. This would mean some change, and the members had accepted it. Indeed, they now were a part of it. He was concerned, however, that the board might conclude with the development of a mission statement—their job being done. According to the book they were all reading, they were off to a good start but there was more to do.

Next comes the crafting of a biblical vision. They needed to decide what God's vision was for their church. This has been problematic for the North American church. Writing in *Leadership*, David Goetz states, "In *Leadership's* study, however, pastors indicated that *conflicting visions for the church* was their greatest source of tension and the top reason they were terminated or forced to resign."[1] Pastor Andy's problem also involved the lack of a vision, which isn't unusual. George Barna writes of pastors that "only 2% could articulate the vision for their church . . . that's one reason so many pastors are ineffective; they don't know where they're going."[2]

At the next board meeting, Andy hesitantly mentioned that they needed a powerful vision statement, expecting some opposition. Much to his surprise, several of the members had already anticipated the need. Their interest had been piqued, and they had read ahead. No one needed to convince them of the importance of a vision. The mission statement had served that purpose.

Both mission and vision are important for essentially the same reasons; however, some confusion existed over the definition of a vision. If Lake Country Church's leadership is to develop a compelling vision for their church, they need to know what a vision is. What is it they're attempting to do? What kinds of visions are there? And how is it different from a mission? This chapter will answer the first two questions; thus defining and determining an organizational, ministry vision. Chapter 7 will answer the third question by delineating the differences between a mission and a vision.

The Definition of a Vision

I define an organizational vision as a clear, challenging picture of the future of the ministry as it can and must be. This definition includes six critical elements.

A Vision Is Clear

The first element of a vision is clarity. It's difficult to accomplish what you don't know. A leader without a clear vision has much in common with a person trying to drive blindfolded. I spent one summer pastoring a seeker church, Crossroads Community Church in Amsterdam, Holland. Since we were so close to France, one weekend my wife and I traveled south to Paris. While there, we visited the Arc de Triomphe. It's a massive, imposing structure that serves as a hub for a number of streets that come together in the heart of Paris. Each street empties into a single street that circles the Arc de Triomphe. You could easily spot the native Parisians from the tourists who attempted to navigate the circular, one-way street. Traffic was constantly attempting to either get on or off the street. For the tourists it was a nightmare. They must have felt that they were on a merry-go-round and couldn't get off. It would have been utter foolishness for a Parisian much less a tourist to attempt to navigate the circle wearing a blindfold.

I believe that a person who attempts to lead a ministry without a vision will have an experience similar to a blindfolded tourist attempting to drive around the Arc de Triomphe. Except for the Scriptures, the only constant in today's world is change. We live in a century wherein everything is changing at breakneck speed. Navigating a ministry vehicle through the last decade of the twentieth century and beyond will prove impossible unless everyone on board knows where that vehicle is headed.

Some ministries do have a vision. The Barna estimate cited previously sets the number of pastors with a vision at 2 percent. But how many of the people in their churches know and understand that vision? If the people who make up a ministry don't understand the vision, then it's not clear. And if it's not clear, then you don't have a vision.

How clear does the vision need to be? I ask pastors what kind of response I would get if I paid an unannounced visit to their church on Sunday morning and asked people what the vision of the church is. I suspect that far too many wouldn't know what I was talking about. Most would refer me back to the pastor. It would be insightful, then, for pastors who have what they think is a clear vision to conduct a vision-clarity test. This involves randomly asking people, including the leaders, what the church's vision is. If the response is silence or a puzzled look, then your vision isn't clear and your work is cut out for you.

Most churches thirst for a biblical vision. I spoke recently with a lay leader of a small church that was without a pastor. Vision was at the top of their list of what they were looking for in a new pastor. Because his church desperately needed clear direction, they were looking for a pastor who was a visionary. While the mission statement provides a ministry with direction, it's the vision statement that creates a clear picture of that direction.

God gave Moses both a clear mission and a clear vision. The mission is found in Exodus 3:10: "So now go. I am sending you to Pharaoh to bring my people the Israelites out of Egypt." This was preceded by Moses' vision in Exodus 3:7–8: "The Lord said, 'I have indeed seen the misery of my people in Egypt. I have heard them crying out because of their slave drivers, and I am concerned about their suffering. So I have come down to rescue them from the hand of the Egyptians and to bring them up out of that land into a good and spacious land, a land flowing with milk and honey—the home of the Canaanites, Hittites, Amorites, Perizzites, Hivites and Jebusites'" (Exod. 3:17). The issue for Moses wasn't vision clarity, it was his confidence in his competence to do that which God had made clear to him (Exod. 3:11).

A Vision Is Challenging

The second element of a vision is that it challenges people. In the Middle Ages, knights wore a flexible metal glove to protect their hands from injury during battle. They called this glove a gauntlet. If the knight wished to challenge someone to personal combat or to express defiance over some issue, it was customary to throw down or take up his gauntlet. This is what a vision does for leaders. It enables them to challenge their people to accomplish great things for the Savior. In short, it inspires or motivates them. This is crucial at a time in North America during which far too many leaders envision throwing in the towel, not throwing down a gauntlet.

It's my firm conviction that pastoring a church is one of the most leadership-intensive tasks that a person could attempt in today's world. This is due primarily to the church's nature as a voluntary, nonprofit organization. It's difficult enough trying to lead people in for-profit organizations. The typical leader has very little leverage in a church because it is a non-profit ministry that depends heavily on volunteers to conduct so much of the ministry.

So, how do you challenge these people? Military leaders can issue orders and marketplace leaders can pay handsomely for people's services. The church has no such leverage. The key is motivating people, and the key to motivation is a clear, challenging vision. Consequently, ministries without a vision are in trouble for there is little else that motivates people to give their lives in service for Christ.

At the end of the 1980s I was reflecting on the vision concept and working with a few churches in the area of vision development. The first church with whom I conducted a vision seminar taught me an important lesson. We spent what we thought was a productive weekend at a comfortable home on a large lake located near Dallas, Texas. We started on Friday evening and finished up Saturday afternoon. Most important was that we had a vision statement to show for all our hard work. One of the leaders had written it down on paper. The task-oriented leadership board was pleased because they had accomplished their goal for the weekend—the development of a church vision statement. The only problem was that when they returned to the church, they filed the vision statement in the church filing cabinet somewhere under *v* and promptly forgot it.

While this church had a so-called vision on paper, they had no vision in practice. The presence of a written document in a filing cabinet "does not a vision make." A good vision challenges the vision designers and the people for whom it's intended. If they're not inspired to implement a God-honoring vision, then they don't have a vision. The document serves only to fill up much-needed space in some church filing cabinet—it challenges and motivates no one.

God's vision for Israel motivated and challenged them. They were in bondage to Egypt. The Egyptians were cruel taskmasters. So cruel that Moses killed one Egyptian because he was beating a Hebrew (Exod. 2:11–13). Then Moses came to Israel with a message of God's freedom and redemption: "And I have promised to bring you up out of your misery in Egypt into the land of the Canaanites, Hittites, Amorites, Perizzites, Hivites and Jebusites—a land flowing with milk and honey." (Exod. 3:17). There was a stark contrast between the harsh condition of making bricks for slave masters in a foreign land and living in your own land that overflowed with milk and honey. Once Moses cast God's vision for his people, they were so challenged that they bowed down and worshiped God (Exod. 4:31).

A Vision Is a Picture

The third vital element is that a vision is a mental picture. As passion is a "feeling" word, so vision is a "seeing" word. In his foreword to *Developing a Vision for the Twenty-first Century*, Haddon Robinson tells the story of someone who shortly after the completion of Disney World said to Mike Vance, the director of Disney Studios, "Isn't it too bad that Walt Disney didn't live to see this!" To which the director replied, "He did see it—that's why it's here."[3]

One of my former students sent me a cartoon that illustrates this point well. The title for the cartoon is "Frog Pioneers." It consists of three frogs wearing coon-skin hats with shovels resting on their shoulders. They're standing in the middle of a desert next to a giant cactus. The caption above one frog's head reads, "We'll put the swamp here!" A vision paints a picture of what tomorrow will look like. Your vision for your ministry is what you see in your head when you close your eyes and picture your ministry two, five, ten, even twenty years from now.

Visionary leaders have a mental picture of what the transcendent, contemporary God has in mind for his people today. They carry in their mental billfolds a visual snapshot of what God can do in their ministries. When they walk through a community, whether located in the throes of poverty in the inner city or the spate of new homes in the suburbs, they don't see just houses or people. They see opportunities for the Savior. They envision places where they can plant churches and people to whom they can minister.

As a seminary professor, I have the privilege of training seminarians as future leaders. As a pastor and church consultant, I also have the honor of training pastors and leadership teams in the context of their ministries. Much of this training is in the area of leadership in general and vision development in particular. Leaders need to take time out of their schooling or busy ministries and dream about the future. They are to picture in their minds what God can do in and through them. As various pictures and images come to mind, I encourage them to write them down.

Not every person is a visionary. God has created some to be visionaries and others to be practical realists. The body of Christ needs both. The visionaries are the more intuitive people who focus on future ideas and what could be, while realists are those who focus on present reality and what is. Those who would lead ministries from the point position should be visionaries. Those who aren't visionaries usually function best in a support position.

You can find out which you are by taking the Myers-Briggs Type Indicator (MBTI) test. It has two preferences that represent both of the above. The intuitive is the visionary; the sensing is the nonvisionary. I should add that while sensing-type people are not natural visionaries, this doesn't mean that they can't catch a vision. They just have to go about doing it a different way because it doesn't come naturally to them; they have to go and see the vision to grasp it. For example, if you're a visionary pastor with a nonvisionary board, then you'll need to take these people to visit a church that has your same vision. They will literally see the vision through their own eyes and hear it through their ears and come to understand what you've been saying.

An important aspect of God's vision for Israel was that they could see their future in the Promised Land. It was to be a future of prosperity—a land flowing with milk and honey. God used his servant Moses to cast and recast this vision throughout the Pentateuch. In one such incident in Deuteronomy 8:7–10, the picture of their future is even more graphic. Moses says: "For the LORD your God is bringing you into a good land— a land with streams and pools of water, with springs flowing in the valleys and hills; . . . a land with wheat and barley, vines and fig trees, pomegranates, olive oil and honey; a land where bread will not be scarce and you will lack nothing; a land where the rocks are iron and you can dig copper out of the hills." The purpose was to provide the Israelites with a mental picture of what their future life would be like.

A Vision Is the Ministry's Future

The fourth element of vision is that it concerns the future. It's a clear description of your ministry's preferred future. It's a mental picture of what tomorrow will look like. It depicts the kind of ministry that you desire yours to become. It's an expression of all your hopes and dreams for your church or parachurch ministry; therefore, when you develop an organizational vision for your ministry, you are thinking about its future.

The older, traditional churches of North America aren't doing well at the end of the twentieth century and the beginning of the third millennium. Lyle Schaller indicates that "two thirds to three fourths of all congregations founded before 1960 are either on a plateau in size or shrinking in numbers."[4] One of the reasons for their decline is that they function as if they are living in the 1940s and 1950s. Their ministry minds are focused on the past when America was a Christian-friendly

quo—it's unacceptable—and a clear grasp of and desire for a better alternative. President John F. Kennedy summed it up well when he said, "Some people see things the way they are and ask why; I see things the way they could be and ask why not?"

In my ministry of teaching and consulting, I find that most ministries err in one of two directions concerning feasibility. The first is that the majority think too small; they have little or no vision. This is often true of seminarians. When they complete their studies, they tend to think too small about their future ministries. One reason is that so many have little ministry experience before coming to seminary, and they spend their time in seminary primarily in the classroom or the library. Thus, they aren't sure of their ministry competence. The questions they ask are: Can I lead? Can I preach? Can I do ministry well? When one questions his or her competence, this adversely affects confidence and diminishes vision.

I find that things aren't that different in the actual ministry world. The churches sprinkled all across North America are going though a period of change. Many small churches are dying while the larger churches are growing bigger. The old-timers in the small churches are hanging in there in spite of the changing communities all around. However, their children aren't proving as faithful; many attend the larger churches with broader ministry menus and more to offer their kids. If you ask the faithful about their vision, their response is, "Huh? We're just trying to keep the doors open!"

This isn't anything new to the ministry world. In Ephesians 3:20, Paul appears to slap the first century church at Ephesus on the wrist for a lack of vision. At the end of his benediction that begins in verse 14, he says, "Now to him who is able to do exceedingly abundantly beyond all that we ask or think . . ." (KJV). He seems to be mildly scolding them for not asking big enough or thinking big enough. This raises the obvious question: What are you praying for and what do you envision? How big are your prayers and dreams?

The Savior was impressed by men and women of strong faith. In Matthew 8, a centurion asked Jesus to heal his servant. This was a man with much power under the Roman military system who believed, however, that he was unworthy of Jesus' presence (v. 8). His humble request was that Jesus simply speak because he was convinced that his words would heal his servant. Matthew records the Savior's response in verse 10: "When Jesus heard this, he was astonished and said to those following him, 'I tell you the truth, I have not found anyone in Israel with such great faith.'"

Jesus periodically rebuked the disciples for not having enough faith. On one occasion, the disciples were worried about their daily need of food and clothing (Matt. 6:25–34). He sadly responds to their lack of trust with the words, "Oh you of little faith." This is important because faith and vision walk hand in hand. Those with little faith most often have little vision. Those with much faith usually display much vision. Consequently, if you want to dream greater dreams, then work on your faith.

While it is rare, the other error is to think too big. The problem is that a vision can be so large that it overwhelms the people in the ministry. When a vision is too big, it intimidates people and dries up their ministry energy before they get started. A sense of futility prevails, and, in time, people drop out of the church. How can you know if your vision is too big? Consider these questions: First, who is the leader, the visionary? Is that person just out of seminary with little if any ministry experience? Is he or she a proven leader who has led other churches or ministries with high impact? Second, who are the followers? Are these people capable of realizing the vision? It's not the leader but his or her followers who carry out the vision. Do these people have the necessary training, gifts, and desire to realize the vision? Finally, is the time right for this vision? Some leaders are way out in front of the times. They anticipate the future so far in advance that the culture or the ministry isn't yet ready for their vision. Other leaders may have fallen behind the times. The world has passed them by and they don't know it. A third group are on top of the times. Like the men of Issachar in the Old Testament, they know how to exegete the culture and are aware of what is taking place around them and how to minister to people (1 Chron. 12:32).

A Vision Must Be

The sixth element is a critical sense of urgency. Not only does the visionary believe that the vision can be, he or she is convinced that it must be. It's more than feasible; the future and, in some cases, the survival of the ministry depend on it.

What fuels this sense of urgency in the visionary? The answer is passion. The visionary is passionate over the vision. He or she feels very strongly about it. The disparity between what is and what could be ignites a passion in the leader's heart. It compels him or her to turn this vision into reality. Ken Hemphill, a seminary president, writes, "Vision is not what ignites growth, it's passion. Burden creates passion. Passion fuels vision, and vision is the focus of the power of passion. I've discovered in churches that leaders who are passionate about their calls create vision."[5]

Several variables contribute to this passion for the vision. One is that God is behind it. He is the source and he is responsible for it. It's his vision for this time and this ministry. Nehemiah sensed this when in

visions. This will help them and those who might join them in ministry to envision what they're doing. Developing a departmental mission helps each to *know* specifically what they're doing and where they're going. Developing a departmental vision helps them *see* what they're doing and where they're going. A departmental vision statement paints a mental picture of what their departments will look like as they realize their individual missions, which will strongly challenge and inspire them to be intentional about accomplishing their dreams for the future.

Notes

1. David L. Goetz, "Forced Out," *Leadership* 17 (Winter 1996): 42.
2. George Barna, "The Man Who Brought Marketing to Church," *Leadership* 16 (Summer 1995): 125.
3. Haddon Robinson, Foreword to *Developing a Vision for Ministry in the Twenty-first Century,* by Aubrey Malphurs (Grand Rapids: Baker, 1992).
4. Randy Frazee and Lyle Schaller, *The Comeback Congregation* (Nashville: Abingdon, 1995), 11.
5. Ken Hemphill, *Southwestern News* (November/December 1994).

7
The Definition of Vision - Part 2
What Is the Difference Between
a Mission and a Vision?

While working their way through the mission development process, one of the board members of Lake Country Church who worked for a Fortune 500 company asked a profound question: What's the difference between a vision and a mission? He had read articles that used both terms, often synonymously. He had also attended various corporate seminars where consultants bandied such terms about. Pastor Andy sensed some differences and briefly elaborated on them off the top of his head, but the question caught him off guard because he wasn't clear on the difference, and he let the members know it. He felt that as a leader he should know such things. He would have felt good to have had an answer ready for such an important question.

This book recognizes an obvious, clear distinction between mission and vision; it treats them separately in parts 2 and 3. In my work with these ideas, various leaders have asked me the same question. Consequently, I make a point in my initial presentation of the vision to detail these differences in anticipation of the question. The mission and the vision have some qualities in common and some that are distinct. The latter outnumber the former. This chapter will help Pastor Andy and other leaders understand these concepts more fully by detailing first their similarities and then their differences.

The Similarities Between a Mission and a Vision

The vision and mission have no less than four common elements. Both find their source in God. Both are future focused. Both are direction oriented. Both are function directed. Pastor Andy, and most likely you

of direction. The mission statement describes the destination. Like a brochure lying on the desk in a travel agency, it tells those planning a trip where they're going. People in a church can read it on the cover of a bulletin or on a wallet-size card or mounted on a wall plaque in the foyer. The vision statement shows people the destination. Like a poster on an agency's wall, it provides a picture. The people in the ministry can see its vision in a sermon, in the life of its leaders, or in a well-prepared video.

The Mission and the Vision Are Function Directed

Both a ministry's mission and its vision are function directed. They address and answer the critical *function* question: What does God want us to do? The mission is a statement of the church or parachurch organization's function. Thus, for the local church that mission is quite clear—make disciples. Whether the church understands its function or not, it still remains the same—to move people to Christlikeness. That's what is involved in making disciples. It must function in such a way that individuals move from wherever they are—lost or saved—to where God wants them to be—mature and Christlike.

Whereas the mission for the church is a statement of the function of disciple making, the vision provides a picture of what a disciple looks like. Lay people are delighted to have a mission statement. They know that you can't focus on fog, and the mission statement blows away the fog so that they can know where the home port or final destination is. But they also want to know what a disciple looks like. What are the behavioral traits of an authentic disciple? And it's the vision, not the mission, that answers this question.

The Differences Between a Mission and a Vision

Now that we've discovered the similarities between the vision and mission, it's time to look at how they are different. I focus attention on twelve major distinctions (see chart 7.1).

1. The Definition

One difference between the mission and vision is found in the definition. You'll recall from chapter 4 that I defined the mission as a broad, brief, biblical statement of what the ministry is supposed to be doing. A key, distinguishing word is *statement*. It is the crucial noun of the definition because it takes several modifiers such as broad, brief, and biblical. The phrase *of what the ministry is supposed to be doing* is also a modifier. Consequently, you see how strategic and crucial *statement* is to the definition. It is a declaration, an expression, or a clarification of the ministry's function.

The vision is different from the mission. In chapter 6 I defined the vision as a clear, challenging picture of the future of the ministry as you believe it can and must be. A key, distinguishing term in the definition of vision is *picture*. It is a key word that is strategic to the definition. The vision is a mental picture, not a statement, of the ministry's direction and function. It's a snapshot that those in the ministry may carry in their mental purses and wallets. It's a portrait of all that God intends the church or parachurch organization to be. And it's the leader's responsibility as a gifted artist to paint for his or her people that portrait.

2. The Application

Another difference is application. The word *application* refers to the primary use of these two concepts. The primary application of the mission is in planning and strategy. It's vital to plan where the ministry organization is going and strategize how to get there. Application is a planning tool. The mission should appear at the beginning of your planning document. The plan is dependent on and grows out of this overall goal.

Ministries that don't plan for their futures have no futures. Some argue that because change is now a constant, planning any further than five or six years ahead is futile. I agree. Today's trends and realities will be different in five years. However, don't interpret this statement to mean that you should jettison planning all together. Should you fail to plan, then you lose control of your future.

Planning in general, and strategizing in particular, is the responsibility of the senior pastor in a church or the president of a parachurch institution. Unfortunately, few seminaries and other institutions for training future leaders prepare their people for this critical function, yet it's essential to an effective ministry in the twenty-first century.

The primary application of the vision is communication. The mission statement also communicates to some degree, but that isn't its primary function. The mission is vital to planning where the church is going, and the vision is vital to communicating the same. It's a communication tool. It becomes the pastor's or primary leader's responsibility to communicate or mold the vision. He or she functions in a ministry as the "keeper of the vision." This involves cultivating (initiating and crafting), communicating (regularly casting and recasting), and clarifying (focusing and fine tuning) the dream for the people.

3. The Length

A third distinction between the mission and the vision is length. The mission statement is shorter than the vision statement. The best mission statements are one sentence in length. And this sentence must be short

informs the head. The emotions hold sway over the intellect. This involves how we feel about what God has directed us to do. The vision helps you to feel strongly about directives such as the Great Commission. It introduces an element of passion into the logical world of obedience. You are moved not only by your intellect or knowledge of what God wants you to do but also by your desire and passion to accomplish it.

7. The Order

A seventh distinction is order. The order involves determining which comes first, the mission or the vision. To some extent this is the same question as: Which comes first, the chicken or the egg? The point is that different people have different experiences and answer accordingly. Some have a vision of God's preferred future for their churches and later adopt a mission. Others begin with a mission and then develop a vision.

A vision is what the organization will look like as it realizes and accomplishes its mission in its ministry area. According to this definition, the organization must first know its mission. Then it moves on and considers its vision. The mission must exist before the vision or there will be no vision. From a logical and developmental perspective, the mission precedes the vision.

One way to develop a vision statement is to begin with the mission statement because it usually comes first. It's shorter and easier to develop first and then expand into the vision. This is a logical approach. First, you develop a mission statement. Next, you take the mission statement and ask: What will this look like as we accomplish it in our ministry community? If your ministry is a church, and its vision is the Great Commission, then what will your community look like as your church pursues, wins, and then disciples these people?

8. The Coherence

An eighth difference is coherence. In this context, coherence refers to how close together something is. It concerns unity, harmony, and agreement.

The missions of most ministry organizations are fairly common. Their mission statements will have more coherence than their vision statements. This is true in particular of the church. Those churches that follow Christ's directive have as their mission the Great Commission. While different churches will articulate the Commission in different ways, the essence is the same. If you were to make a list of fifteen or twenty biblical church-mission statements, all would be slightly different. However, at the center of each would be the Great Commission mission.

The visions of most ministries, however, will be unique. Though the mission is common, the communities in which they are realized are not.

Every community is different. The community may be inner-city, suburban, or rural. The ethnic makeup of the area may be predominantly Hispanic, African American, Asian, or Anglo. It may be affluent while another is poverty stricken. The community may consist of well-educated people while another consists of the uneducated. The vision filtered through a unique community will reflect these differences and will not be coherent from church to church.

9. The Focus

A ninth distinction is focus. The mission has a broad focus. Its purpose is to give the overview or the big picture. When people hear the mission, they have the broad umbrella that covers the ministry. If you were filming your church or parachurch ministry, the camera would back off and shoot from a distance in order to capture the mission.

The vision's focus is narrow. If you were filming your ministry's vision, the camera would move in close. A vision provides a picture of what Christ wants you to do. Pictures provide details. You look at a group shot of several people and you see distinctions such as different faces, clothes, and so on. Your vision will include such distinctions. If you are targeting an inner-city community, then you might see the poor and oppressed. If you have targeted a blue-collar community, then you will see people wearing blue jeans as opposed to a coat and tie.

10. The Effect

A tenth difference is effect. The effect refers to the result or consequence that the mission or vision has on people. The effect of the mission is to clarify for all what they are supposed to be doing. There are numerous trails that a ministry could take through the ministry maze. Some ministries, for example, are walking down the education trail. They see as their mission educated Christians—those who know their Bibles. Others are walking the evangelism trail. They exist to win souls. Still others are hiking across the social trail. They exist to help the disenfranchised and downcast. It is the mission that determines the organization's distinct ministry trail. This is a mission's clarifying effect.

The effect of the vision isn't to clarify the organization's direction and function. To some extent it may do this; as people begin to see where they're going, some clarification will take place. However, the vision effect is to challenge. Once the leadership has clarified what they're supposed to be doing, the vision challenges them to do it. Both are necessary. Knowing where you're going and getting there aren't the same. Your people may need some initial and long-term help in moving toward where they know they're supposed to be going. The vision serves this purpose. As people envision where the ministry can

2. How do you plan to apply your vision statement to your church or parachurch ministry? Will you use it primarily for planning or communication?
3. How long is your vision statement? Is it longer than, the same size as, or shorter than your mission statement?
4. What is the purpose of your vision statement? Have you developed it primarily to inform or inspire your people?
5. What kind of activity does your vision promote—doing or seeing?
6. What was the source of your vision? Did it come from what God put on your heart or in your head?
7. While it's not a final determiner of your vision, which came first, your vision or your mission?
8. At the core, does your vision have much in common with most other visions that you know of, or is it unique?
9. How focused is your vision? Is it very broad or is it detailed? Does it give you the big picture or does it provide many of the details?
10. What primary effect does your vision have on your people? Does it clarify for them where you're going and what you're supposed to be doing, or does it challenge them to the same?
11. In the development of your vision, was it more caught or taught? How long did it take you to develop it?
12. As a leader and communicator, what have you found to be the best way to communicate your vision to your followers—visually or verbally?

8

The Development of a Vision
How to Birth Your Vision

Pastor Andy and the members on the board read the chapter in their ministry basics book that distinguishes between a mission and a vision. After they had discussed the chapter and its distinctions, all felt good about their mission statement and most were ready and eager to pursue the development of a church vision. Harry Smith was the only person who expressed any reluctance. He raised several insignificant questions that some of the older members on the board handled admirably well. After that, he seemed cautiously willing to move forward. The spirit of the board was such, however, that they didn't leave him much choice.

They decided that Pastor Andy would draft an initial vision statement and bring it to the board for their perusal. Their confidence in him and his abilities pleased Andy. He viewed this as an expression of their confidence in him as a leader. At the same time, he knew that developing a vision for their church would be more difficult than developing the mission had been. Because a vision is caught, he hoped that he would catch it well. Although his recent success with the mission statement had catalyzed his optimism, he saw a vision statement as a challenge to be met head on.

How do you birth a vision? What steps should Pastor Andy and the board take to develop a clear challenging vision for Lake Country Church? The answer is the three *p*s: the personnel, the process, and the product. The personnel are those who roll up their sleeves and do the actual vision work. The process will guide you through the steps for vision development. The section on product will provide you with several sample vision statements that are not only the result of the process but will also prove instructive.

to be regularly updated and fine-tuned. This is because the ministry circumstances will change as the organization begins to implement the vision in a changing world. The vision will become clearer and more defined as problems surface and victories are won.

Significant Others

If the cultivation of the vision is the primary domain of the point person, what is the role of the others on the ministry team? How will they gain ownership of the vision if they're not significantly involved? If Pastor Andy is primarily responsible to develop the vision, what should he expect from his board? Will the board members feel that the vision is theirs if they don't have their fingerprints all over it?

A common assumption in leadership circles is that a vision is the key to the success of a ministry. Most conversations on leadership today are punctuated with the *vision* word. While vision is important, it's not the only key. You have learned in this book that there are other "keys" to ministry such as your values and your mission.

I believe that mission is as important if not more important than vision; however, with all the current emphasis and hype on vision, we have lost the value and importance of a well-defined and well-articulated ministry mission. We must get the two into perspective. As I have arranged them in this book, the mission is critical to the vision. It logically precedes and gives birth to the vision.

Therefore, the place where the board provides leadership and input and gains ownership is in the development of the ministry's mission. You don't have to be a visionary to develop a mission, but the point leader must not develop the mission alone. He needs to involve significant others in the process and their involvement, in turn, provides them with ownership. It allows them to get their fingerprints all over the ministry mission and the church's future.

Once a board senses that it has had a great impact on the organization's future and that it owns that future in the form of a mission statement, not as much involvement in the development of the vision is required. The crafting of the vision creates a picture of the ministry's future—a future that they have had a major part in determining. This dream challenges people to move toward that picture, and it's okay to let another, an artist, paint this for them and the ministry.

So what is the role of the board in developing the vision? Their role is one of cooperation, support, and communication.

Cooperation. They must cooperate with and follow the leadership of a visionary point leader. They must recognize that this person is a gifted visionary and may, therefore, see things that they can't see (if they are nonvisionaries) or don't see (if they are visionaries). They must avoid power plays, self-interests, and private agendas. They must put God and his ministry first if they are to have a compelling biblical vision.

Support. They must support the visionary leader and his or her effort to develop a significant vision. Cooperation and support aren't the same. You may cooperate with someone but not support them. This is difficult, but it can be done. What they need, however, is your support. You must be behind them and the effort. If you aren't, other board members and people within the organization will sense it and may not support the effort as well. This could prove disastrous. I suggest that if you can't support the visionary point leader, then you should move to another situation where you can. Otherwise, you do harm to the ministry as well as to yourself.

Communication. While the visionary point person has the primary responsibility to articulate and cast the vision, the significant others need to be doing the same. Vision casting isn't the exclusive role of the primary leader. The ministry community needs to hear the vision in many different ways from as many different people as possible. They should tell what they see as they envision the accomplishment of the mission in the ministry community. However, they must listen carefully as the primary leader casts the vision to make sure that they aren't contradicting what he or she says. Individual vision casting not only communicates the vision but also communicates that the leadership supports the vision. Your people can cast the dream one-on-one, in small-group meetings, and in town-hall meetings.

The Vision Development Process

Now that you know who the primary vision person is, the next question is: How does that person craft the vision? What process should you or Pastor Andy follow? It consists of two steps.

Expand the Mission Statement

The best way to develop a powerful, challenging vision is to expand the mission statement. This assumes that you have followed the order in this book (values, mission, vision, and strategy) and have developed the mission statement first. Start with the completed mission statement. Then you should ask: What will the ministry look like as it accomplishes this mission in its ministry context or community?

You may attempt to construct a vision without a mission statement. Some become so intent on developing a vision for their ministry that they skip all the earlier chapters of a book such as this and turn straight to the chapter on vision development. This is not the best way. With others, however, the vision simply happens. They think and pray about their ministry and suddenly a picture pops into their heads. I suspect that this is the direct or indirect act of God.

God's Vision Statement for Israel

The first is God's vision for his people as communicated through Moses. This becomes Moses' vision statement for Israel. In chapter 4, I presented Moses' mission statement: "So now go. I am sending you to Pharaoh to bring my people the Israelites out of Egypt" (Exod. 3:10). This mission is expanded in God's vision for his people: "So I have come down to rescue them from the hand of the Egyptians and to bring them up out of that land into a good and spacious land, a land flowing with milk and honey—the home of the Canaanites, Hittites, Amorites, Perizzites, Hivites, and Jebusites" (Exod. 3:8). Moses will cast and recast this vision in a number of places as recorded throughout the Pentateuch (Exod. 13:5; Deut. 8:7–9; 11:9). Noteworthy is Deuteronomy 8:7–9:

> For the Lord your God is bringing you into a good land—a land with streams and pools of water, with springs flowing in the valleys and hills; a land with wheat and barley, vines and fig trees, pomegranates, olive oil and honey; a land where bread will not be scarce and you will lack nothing; a land where the rocks are iron and you can dig copper out of the hills.

Moses simply expands the mission statement. He creates a vivid picture of what their future life will look like and be like in the Promised Land. You can enter somewhat into the experience of the Israelite as you hear this vision. You can't help seeing streams and pools of water, wheat and barley waving in the breeze, trees with luscious figs, and ripe pomegranates. You can almost taste the honey and feel its stickiness between your fingers. You can smell the fresh bread baking in the oven.

Martin Luther King Jr.'s Vision for America

Another vision statement and one of the most famous in recent American history is the vision of Martin Luther King Jr. While it depicts what he saw when he envisioned the future of African Americans in this country, it also pictures what he saw when he envisioned every American's future. It's his vision for America.

> I say to you today, my friends, that in spite of the difficulties and frustrations of the moment I still have a dream. It is a dream deeply rooted in the American dream.
> I have a dream that one day this nation will rise up and live out the true meaning of its creed: "We hold these truths to be self-evident; that all men are created equal."
> I have a dream that one day on the red hills of Georgia the

sons of former slaves and the sons of former slave owners will be able to sit down together at the table of brotherhood.

I have a dream that one day even the state of Mississippi, a desert state sweltering with the heat of injustice and oppression, will be transformed into an oasis of freedom and justice.

I have a dream that my four little children will one day live in a nation where they will be judged not by the color of their skin but by the content of their character.

I have a dream today. I have a dream that one day the state of Alabama, whose governor's lips are presently dripping with the words of interposition and nullification, will be transformed into a situation where little black boys and black girls will be able to join hands with little white boys and white girls and walk together as sisters and brothers.

I have a dream today. I have a dream that one day every valley shall be exalted, every hill and mountain shall be made low, the rough places will be made plains, and the crooked places will be made straight, and the glory of the Lord shall be revealed, and all flesh shall see it together.

This is our hope. This is the faith with which I return to the South. With this faith we will be able to transform the jangling discords of our nation into a beautiful symphony of brotherhood. With this faith we will be able to work together, to pray together, to struggle together, to go to jail together, to stand up for freedom together, knowing that we will be free one day.

This will be the day when all God's children will be able to sing with new meaning, "My country 'tis of thee, sweet land of liberty, of thee I sing. Land where my fathers died, land of the pilgrim's pride, from every mountainside, let freedom ring."

And if America is to be a great nation this must become true. So let freedom ring from the prodigious hilltops of New Hampshire. Let freedom ring from the mighty mountains of New York. Let freedom ring from the heightening Alleghenies of Pennsylvania! Let freedom ring from the snowcapped Rockies of Colorado! Let freedom ring from the curvaceous peaks of California! But not only that; let freedom ring from the Stone Mountain of Georgia! Let freedom ring from every hill and molehill of Mississippi. From every mountainside, let freedom ring.

When we let freedom ring, when we let it ring from every village and every hamlet, from every state and every city, we will be able to speed up that day when all of God's children, black men and white men, Jews and Gentiles, Protestants and

It is the dream of a place where the hurting, the depressed, the frustrated, and the confused can find love, acceptance, help, hope, forgiveness, guidance, and encouragement.

It is the dream of sharing the Good News of Jesus Christ with the hundreds of thousands of residents in south Orange County.

It is the dream of welcoming 20,000 members into the fellowship of our church family—loving, learning, laughing, and living in harmony together.

It is the dream of developing people to spiritual maturity through Bible studies, small groups, seminars, retreats, and a Bible school for our members.

It is the dream of equipping every believer for a significant ministry by helping them discover the gifts and talents God gave them.

It is the dream of sending out hundreds of career missionaries and church workers all around the world, and empowering every member for a personal life mission in the world. It is the dream of sending our members by the thousands on short-term mission projects to every continent. It is the dream of starting at least one new daughter church every year.

It is the dream of at least fifty acres of land, on which will be built a regional church for south Orange County—with beautiful, yet simple, facilities including a worship center seating thousands, a counseling and prayer center, classrooms for Bible studies and training lay ministers, and a recreation area. All of this will be designed to minister to the total person—spiritually, emotionally, physically, and socially—and set in a peaceful inspiring garden landscape.

I stand before you today and state in confident assurance that these dreams will become reality. Why? Because they are inspired by God![4]

Pastor Rick Warren has taken a topical approach to vision development. Each paragraph presents his dream on a particular topic affecting the future of the church. There are seven. The first is his vision for people—the hurting, depressed, and so on. The second topic is evangelism—"sharing the Good News of Jesus Christ." The third is members or the church family. Note that here he sets a numerical goal of twenty thousand members. The fourth topic is his dream for his church's spiritual maturity accompanied by a strategy. The fifth topic is lay involvement or empowerment—it is his vision to equip all of his people for ministry. The sixth is missions—the sending out of lay and career missionaries all over the world. The final topic is land and facilities that will contribute to the development of the total person. Note that the second through sixth topics are vital parts of the Saddleback strategy.

As a visionary, Rick Warren took these various topics and dreamed about them. As in this case, when pictures came to mind he both preached them and wrote them down. Essentially, Rick expanded each topic into a full-blown picture of what the church would look like in the future. He may have done this by design, or it may have simply come to mind, as happens with visionaries.

Tim Armstrong's Vision for Crossroads Community Church

Tim Armstrong is a graduate of Dallas Seminary. During his last year of seminary, he initiated the planting of Crossroads Community Church near Mansfield, Ohio. The following is his vision for this church:

> The writer of Proverbs wrote, "Where there is no vision the people perish" (29:18). At Crossroads, it is our desire that you catch the vision God has given us, that you begin to visualize the invisible! We have worked hard at defining our vision so that it is clear, challenging, and concise. It is our desire that you clearly see the future of the ministry—what it can be and what it must be. But most importantly, we want you to capture the concept of our vision so that it will capture you and provide a foundation for your personal ministry with us at Crossroads.
>
> In part, the vision of Crossroads Community Church is to become a biblically functioning community. This will become clear as you continue through the notebook. However, our complete vision statement more specifically defines our desires.
>
> ### Crossroads Vision Statement
> The vision of Crossroads Community Church is to creatively implement the Great Commission to build a growing community of churches around the perimeter of Mansfield by planting culturally relevant churches every three years that are committed to dynamic worship of God while extending His transforming grace to reach the unchurched community.
>
> There are five key phrases that outline our vision. They represent the core of our vision and are essential for evaluating, re-defining, and sharpening our focus. The five key phrases are:

Reach the Unchurched

Finally, our vision includes the intentional pursuit of reaching those who have stopped attending, or have never attended a church. In other words, those who have not experienced God's transforming grace.

Placing a vision in print is somewhat like attempting to hold water in your hand. It is nearly impossible! A vision is something that is caught rather than taught. Vision has been described as a mental picture of the future that finds its realization in the hands of the one who owns the vision. It is our desire that the Crossroads vision becomes your vision; something you "own" and take great pride in seeing fulfilled. In essence, our vision is not something that you can see, but something you must be.

After a two-paragraph introduction, Pastor Tim Armstrong presents a full, one sentence vision statement. It consists of a "what" and a "how." The what is to implement the Great Commission around the perimeter of Mansfield, Ohio. The how is to plant churches, and the first is Crossroads Community Church of Ontario, Ohio. Then he lifts "five key phrases" out of the statement and expands each.

You should note the practice of expanding in vision drafting. Earlier I stated that the best way to craft a ministry vision is to begin with a mission statement. Once you've developed the mission, then you develop your vision by expanding that mission statement. This has proved true of all the vision statements above. Here, Pastor Tim begins with a statement that some would say is his mission statement. I would describe it as a minivision statement because it consists of his mission (the what) and strategy (the how). Regardless, it contains the essential ingredients of his vision. All that remains is for him to dream and picture what each of these ingredients will look like as the church realizes its mission and strategy. In this vision statement, he has chosen to write down, for his people and potential members, what he sees.

Bill Hybels' Vision for Willow Creek Community Church

Bill Hybels is the senior pastor of Willow Creek Community Church that is located in Barrington, Illinois, just west of Chicago. On numerous occasions over the twenty-year history of Willow Creek, Hybels has cast and recast his vision for the church. The most recent was during "Vision Night 96." This vision event was very strategic in the life of the church because it marked their twenty-year anniversary and set the course of the church for the next five years.

It's not feasible to include Hybel's sermon here. In summary, he crafted the entire sermon around the church's strategic plan for the next five years. In this sermon, he conveys the plan and describes what he sees as he pictures Willow Creek's future in the Chicago area. The vision talk communicates three major goals or what Hybel's calls three "big ideas" or "values." The first goal is: "We feel we need to reach an ever-increasing percentage of the Chicago-land area with the Gospel message." The second is: "We are going to move the congregation of Christ followers toward community, spiritual maturity, and full participation in the life of the church." And the last goal is: "We are going to invest a greater percentage of our lives and our knowledge and our resources with those in our city, our nation, and our world."

Next, he elaborates on the strategy or how the church plans to accomplish each of these big ideas. Many of them affect their programs. For example, the church will implement the first evangelistic goal by training members in evangelism, inviting seekers to a weekend service and to the small-group meetings, conducting outreach concerts, and helping other churches in the community to become evangelistically intense.

Third, Hybels announces that the ministry team at Willow Creek has set a numerical figure for each major goal. The figure for the first is to have more than twenty thousand people in attendance at the weekend services. The figure for the second is eight thousand people at the New Community service, and the third is eight thousand people serving in ministries outside Willow Creek. This is a great example of the importance of thinking big as Paul encourages in Ephesians 3:20.

Fourth, someone on the leadership team has taken responsibility for each major goal. They will function as the point person to gather the other leaders around them to make sure that the entire staff and all the leaders of the church are working together toward this goal. For example, Lee Strobel has volunteered to become the point person for the first goal, John Ortburg the second goal, and John Burke the third.

Finally, it's important to vision development and casting to note how Hybels (as well as the others) says what he says. His use of words, phrases, and statements is powerful. He describes the goal of evangelizing Chicago as "an all-out full-court press." He is counting on the witness of the church "to burn brightly." He speaks of taking risks as "being free with and even reckless with" the Gospel. He talks about "evangelistic intensity." He describes the initiation of the program as, "the starting gun goes off and we charge into the future." He hopes that his people will be "contagious Christians." And he's going "to turn up the thermostat at the weekend services."

Questions for Thought and Discussion

1. Will the development of the vision be the primary domain of the ministry leader? Who will be the personnel involved in the drafting

of your ministry's vision? Are these people visionaries or practical realists? How do you know? Have they taken the Myers-Briggs Type Indicator or the Kiersey-Bates Temperament Sorter? Why or why not?

2. How will the other significant people in the ministry contribute to the crafting of the vision? How might the practical realists contribute? How might the other visionaries help?

3. Have you developed the mission before attempting to draft the vision? Why or why not? Have you skipped over the first two parts of this book because someone has convinced you that your primary ministry need is a powerful, significant vision? How will Parts 1 and 2 of this book be beneficial to the crafting of a vision?

4. How much time do you have or plan to spend praying for your vision? Is it or will it be big enough? How do you know? Are you at least verbalizing if not writing down your thoughts as you work through the envisioning process?

5. Is your vision clear? Challenging? Does it prompt pictures in people's minds? Does it focus on the future? Do you believe that your vision is possible? Do you have a passion to see it through to its realization?

6. Why is it important that you go through the envisioning process before adopting a vision? What's wrong, if anything, with using another ministry's vision? Is it okay to put together different parts from other statements to form your own, unique vision?

7. In this chapter, I have presented several vision statements. Which did you like best? What was it that attracted you to it? Which didn't you care for? Why?

8. How will these statements help you in developing your vision? Could you use some or all of them in some way to communicate your vision at various times and at various events in the life of your ministry? Does their use of language help or inspire you in some way?

Notes

1. Most counseling centers can administer this test.
2. David Kiersey and Marilyn Bates, *Please Understand Me* (Del Mar, Calif.: Prometheus Nemesis Book Company, 1978), 5–12.
3. Martin Luther King Jr., "I Have a Dream," in *The Words of Martin Luther King, Jr.,* ed. C. S. Kind (New York: Newmarket Press, 1983), 95–98.
4. Rick Warren, *The Purpose Driven Church* (Grand Rapids: Zondervan, 1995), 43.

Part 4

The Strategy for Your Ministry

9

The Definition of Strategy
What Is a Strategy?

P astor Andy had read that a vision statement wouldn't come overnight. He would have to be patient and give it some time. This bothered him because he didn't feel that the church had a lot of time. He was also a hard charger and wanted to take the "vision hill" soon. At the same time, he believed that if the vision statement was worth developing at all, then he preferred to do it well. So he would trust God to supply him with a superabundance of patience during his vision quest.

He did, however, plan to move ahead with the crafting of a strategy that would implement the church's new mission. According to the ministry basics book he and his board were reading, he didn't have to wait until he completed the vision to begin to work on the strategy. The mission is the key concept. Both the vision and the strategy work off the ministry mission (see figure I.1). And the strategy isn't just any strategy. Every ministry will have a number of strategies: a worship strategy, an evangelism strategy, a small-group's strategy, and others. The topic of this chapter is the ministry's mission strategy. It's the umbrella under which all the other strategies must stand.

Pastor Andy was a novice; he had never developed a mission strategy before. Nothing was said about it in seminary. He realized that Lake Country Church, like all churches, had a strategy that had been in place for years, and though somehow the original mission had been lost, the strategy had survived. But it didn't make much sense without a clear mission. It was a classic case of putting the semi's trailer in front of the tractor.

Now that Lake Country has a mission, it's imperative that the ministry team rethink and develop a clear, high-impact strategy to implement that mission. The strategy is the vehicle that enables the church to bring about its mission. It accomplishes little if the tractor shows up without its trailer. The strategy also helps your people to understand why they're doing what they're doing. Far too many people are going through the motions without understanding. The strategy explains why they attend a worship service, a small group, or a special seminar as well as other events. Finally, a strategy provides a sense of momentum or progress. A good strategy takes its people through the discipleship-development process. This process has clear, discernible steps. As people take those steps, they gain a sense of spiritual momentum—they are going somewhere spiritually. On the one hand, it's encouraging for them to look back and see where they've been. On the other hand, it's challenging for them to see where they have yet to go.

Before Pastor Andy begins to develop his mission strategy, he needs to make sure that he understands what a strategy is. It can prove embarrassing to attempt to do something only to discover that you didn't understand precisely what it was you were attempting to do. The leader orders his followers: "Charge the hill!" and some people pull out their credit cards while others load their guns. How many times have we differed with someone over an issue, only to understand later that we weren't even talking about the same thing? Clear communication is the key. So what is not a strategy? What is a strategy? What kinds of strategy are there?

What a Strategy Is Not

As with the other concepts of this book, I believe that you will best understand the mission strategy if I define what it isn't as well as what it is. Leaders may confuse the strategy with a number of other concepts such as values, mission, and vision. I see this confusion in discussions of these concepts in the marketplace, though a strategy is most commonly confused with a plan.

Although an organizational strategy is commonly equated with an organizational plan, they're not the same. They are often used as synonyms. The problem is that the two have some similarities and some differences. For example, both the plan and the strategy answer the *how* question: How will we charge the hill? How will we accomplish our ministry mission? Their differences, however, far exceed their commonalties.

The strategy is a part of the plan but not the same as the plan. The plan is much broader and subsumes the strategy along with a number of other concepts. One simplified method of planning that I have developed for established churches is found in chart 9.1.

In this model, the strategy is primarily the seventh but also the eighth part of the plan. A plan is one of the ministry ABCs. However, I have chosen not to cover ministry planning as it's too vast a concept for this

1.	Values Audit
2.	Mission Development
3.	Environmental Scan
4.	Vision Development
5.	Performance Audit
6.	Gap Analysis
7.	Strategy Development
8.	Strategy Implementation
9.	Regular Evaluation

Chart 9.1: The Ministry Plan

book, and there are already a number of books available on the topic.[1] The important point is that you see the difference between the strategy and the plan and that you realize that your work isn't complete once you've developed your strategy. Strategy must fit within the context of a ministry plan.

A second distinction is orientation. The strategy is action oriented, not intention oriented. A plan is exactly that—a plan for action. Whereas, a strategy is the action. In a plan, leaders and administrators set forth their ministry goals and objectives. In a strategy, they attempt to accomplish those goals and objectives. Leaders tend to drift toward strategizing; administrators tend to favor planning. A person with the gift of leadership and administration is strong as a primary leader because he or she favors both.

In *Managing the Non-Profit Organization*, Peter Drucker illustrates the distinction: "Good intentions don't move mountains, bulldozers do."[2] Strategies are bulldozers—they're action oriented. Plans are good intentions—they're intention oriented. Drucker states that planning is what you want to do—an intellectual exercise, good intentions. Strategy is your accomplishments. Strategy transforms intentions into actions. It involves not wanting to do something but doing it. In planning, we say that we intend to "take the hill," in strategizing, we "take the hill."

On the surface, these distinctions may seem minor; however, the literature on the subject uses both terms casually. Consequently, you must be careful in the use of terms or reap confusion.

What a Strategy Is

A strategy is the process that determines how you will accomplish the mission of your ministry. This definition has three vital concepts.

A Strategy Has a Mission

First, a strategy must have a mission. According to chapter 4 every ministry must have a mission and should articulate that mission in a mission statement. The crying need in many if not most churches in North America is for them to know where they're going. As one church elder and chairman of the board recently said to me, "We desperately need some direction!"

A church without a mission is like a plane without a destination. I frequently fly out of Love Field in Dallas, Texas. It has many advantages over the huge Dallas-Fort Worth Airport located equidistant between Dallas and Fort Worth. Two of those advantages are proximity to Dallas and ease of parking. I also like to fly Southwest Airlines, which only flies out of Love Field. Southwest is a customer-friendly airline. For example, when you board the flight, often the captain is standing at the door to greet you. I enjoy joking with the pilots. But can you imagine my consternation if I asked him jokingly, "Where are we going?" And he soberly responded, "Beats me, I don't have a clue!" Yet many of our churches when asked where they're going, soberly respond, "We don't have a clue!" Would you climb on board?

What is amazing to me is that all of these churches have a strategy. A church has to have programs to keep its doors open. They have to have something in place for people to come to. The programs are the end product of a strategy. If you examine a ministry's programs, you will learn much about its strategy. Most older, traditional churches for years have followed the three-to-thrive programming concept. They meet Sunday morning for Sunday school and a preaching and worship service. They meet Sunday night for a preaching service. Finally, they meet Wednesday night for prayer. These programs reflect a strategy. The strategy is to teach people God's word, to worship, and to pray.

If you ask these churches why they are doing these important things, however, they blink and become quiet. Some will respond with, "We've always done it that way!" This is true, but it is hardly an adequate answer. What has happened is that the church over the years has lost sight of its mission. When it was founded, the mission was clear. The core group and the planting pastor knew what they were supposed to be doing. They also developed the three-to-thrive strategy to accomplish the mission. Along with the strategy, they implemented the various programs that reflect that strategy.

Over time, the founding pastor left and was followed by other pastors. In the exchange of the pastoral baton, somehow the church misplaced the mission while the programs became hardened tradition. It's tragic that not only did they lose the mission, but the programs reflect America as it was in the 1930s, 1940s, and 1950s. What is wrong with that? The problem is that we no longer live in that time. People have changed and the country has changed. The culture is no longer church friendly. And Christ's church must change and target America's lost and dying unchurched population. They not only are the future of this country, but they are also the future of the church.

Strategy begins by taking part 2 of this book seriously and developing a dynamic, biblical mission. We must determine what God's mission is for our ministry. We must discover what it is that God wants us to do. Pastors and leaders must ask and answer the question: Where is this plane going after it leaves the airport? Once they have a biblical answer, then they must pursue it with a passion. Key to that pursuit is a strategy that is both relevant to and understanding of today's world and the world of tomorrow.

A Strategy Is a Process

A strategy isn't static, it involves a process. It's the process of moving people from prebirth to maturity. Prebirth refers to that period in one's life when he or she is not a Christian. I have labeled it prebirth because it takes place before the new birth (John 3:1–7). The prebirth stage begins at physical birth and lasts up to the new birth. You will find non-Christians at various stages of unbelief during the prebirth period. Some may be far from the Savior, such as Herod (Acts 12:21–23) and Saul (Acts 8:1–3). Others may be seekers and very close to faith as were Nicodemus (John 3), Zacchaeus (Luke 19:3), the Ethiopian eunuch (Acts 8:26), and Cornelius (Acts 10).

The maturity stage begins at new birth (conversion) and lasts until the Christian dies and joins his or her Savior. I use the word *maturity* optimistically. It describes what should happen during this time. The process is for believers to move from new birth to maturity or Christlikeness (Col. 1:28–29; 2:6–7).

According to research done for the Evangelical Free Church in America by Bob Gilliam, this process isn't happening in our churches. He conducted a survey that included four thousand attendees in thirty-five churches in several denominations from Florida to Washington. Gilliam discovered the following:

- There is absolutely no correlation between the length of time a person had been a Christian and their level of maturity.
- Many persons do not understand the meaning of discipleship or the spiritual disciplines. For instance, it is very common for people to report that they did have a regular daily quiet time with God, but in a later question state that they only did this about twice a year.
- Most people in these churches are not growing spiritually. Of those

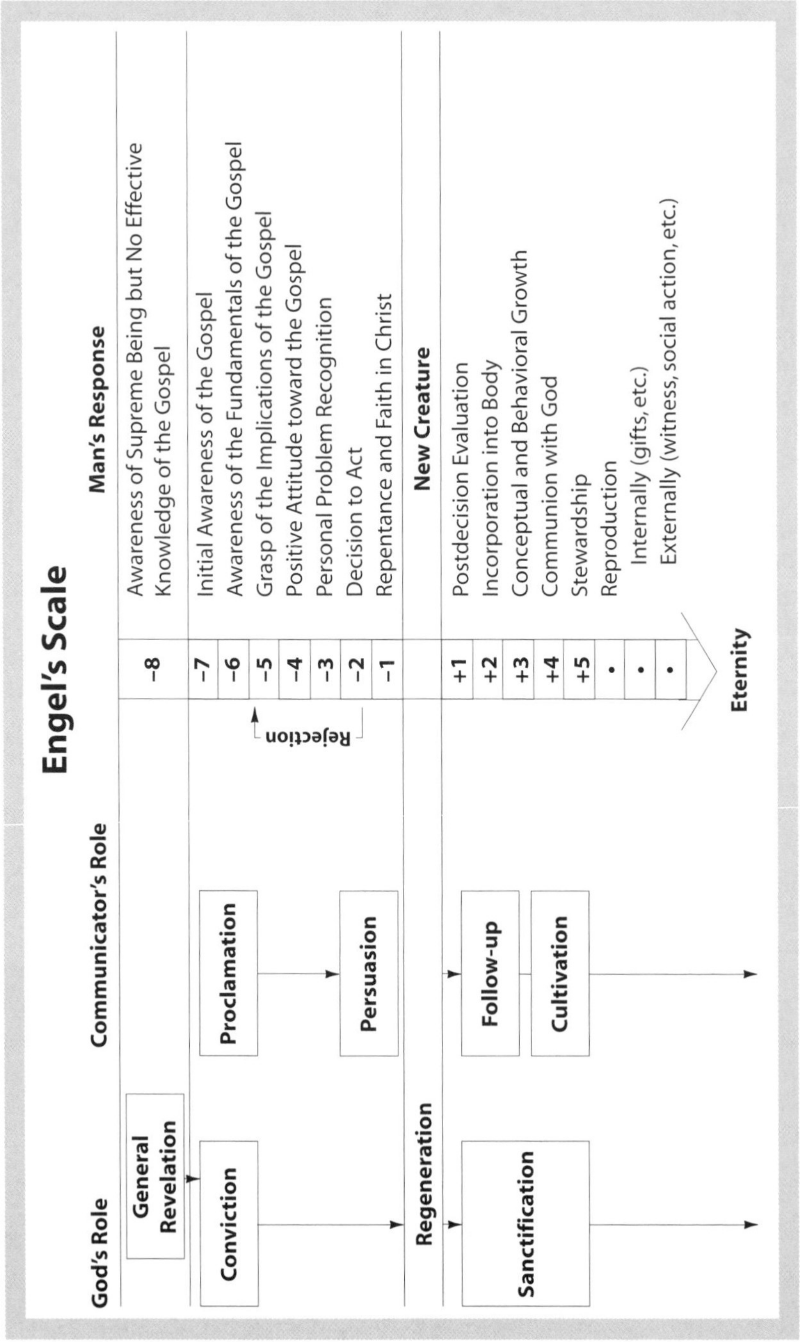

Engel's Scale

God's Role	Communicator's Role	Man's Response	
		Man's Response	
		Awareness of Supreme Being but No Effective Knowledge of the Gospel	-8
General Revelation	**Proclamation**	Knowledge of the Gospel	
Conviction		Initial Awareness of the Gospel	-7
		Awareness of the Fundamentals of the Gospel	-6
		Grasp of the Implications of the Gospel	-5
	Persuasion	Positive Attitude toward the Gospel	-4
		Personal Problem Recognition	-3
		Decision to Act	-2
		Repentance and Faith in Christ	-1
Regeneration		**New Creature**	
	Follow-up	Postdecision Evaluation	+1
		Incorporation into Body	+2
Sanctification	**Cultivation**	Conceptual and Behavioral Growth	+3
		Communion with God	+4
		Stewardship	+5
		Reproduction	
		Internally (gifts, etc.)	•
		Externally (witness, social action, etc.)	•

Rejection

Eternity

Figure 9.1: Engel's Scale

taking the survey, 24 percent indicated that their behavior was sliding backward and 41 percent said they were "static" in their spiritual growth.[3]

The strategy process recognizes that people are at different places in their spiritual journeys. Scripture acknowledges this as well (Matt. 13:18–23). You design the process to move people from wherever they are spiritually (lost or saved) to where God wants them to be (spiritually mature). Therefore, a person in your church or a new person to your ministry will find that the strategy is tailor-made for him or her. There is a program in place for each person.

There are numerous ways to communicate the process. One is to use Engel's Scale (see figure 9.1).[4] This scale is a continuum that represents the process of moving a lost person from one extreme (no knowledge of the Gospel) to the other (witnessing and living for Christ). The steps are conviction, regeneration, and sanctification. This scale helps us to see the process that a person goes through as he or she moves toward faith and then toward maturity.

Another way to communicate the process is to view it as levels of commitment. This is a simple process that your people can easily picture and understand. In this process, your strategy should reflect at least three levels of commitment (see figure 9.2).

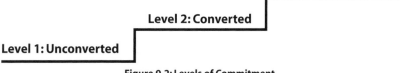

Figure 9.2: Levels of Commitment

Level one is where lost people are. They move to level two when they come to faith. Immediately after they come to faith, the church needs to help them move toward level three (maturity or Christlikeness). When people come to faith in Christ, they are responsible to move from one level to another. And it's the church's responsibility to help them in the process. Studies indicate that if someone doesn't come alongside a new convert, the chances are good that they will fall into nominal Christianity. The object of the church's strategy is to move them from the lowest level to the highest.

A Strategy Answers the Question, How?

Your mission strategy answers a critical question. It asks and answers the *how* question: How will this ministry, whether church or parachurch, accomplish its mission? Strategy is the ministry means to realize the ministry ends. If your mission is to take the hill, then your strategy is the *how* that will move you from the bottom to the top of that hill.

Since every church has a strategy reflected in its programs and activities, when asked these questions, some people comment, "Oh, we already have a strategy." They are correct; however, the important question to ask is: Is it a good strategy? The answer is simple: If it is accomplishing the mission of the ministry, then it's probably a good one. If the answer is, "Huh?" then you're in trouble.

At the end of this century, the majority of the typical, traditional churches still cling to the three-to-thrive strategy that characterized most churches in the first half of the century. If you ask them how they are attempting to accomplish God's mission for them, they will show you their bulletin or a copy of their programs. My experience is that in much of America, especially urban America of the 1990s, strategy has not proved to be disciple friendly. You must regularly ask the *how* question so that your strategy is in tune with where the believers and unbelievers of this generation are.

The Kinds of Strategies

We can further define and refine the definition of a strategy by examining three different kinds of strategies.

The Personal Strategy

In chapter 4 I pointed out that Christians should develop a personal life mission that answers the question: What does God want to accomplish in and through my life? The answer determines what you will do with your life and how you'll serve Christ. My personal ministry mission is to equip a new generation of leaders all over the world for significant, high-impact ministry in the twenty-first century. This mission statement helps me to make decisions that affect my life. When ministry opportunities come my way, I decide whether to pursue them based on my ministry mission. It also helps me to be proactive in ministry rather than reactive. Through God's strength and guidance, I shape my life and ministry rather than allow other people and other events to do so. Your personal strategy relates directly to your personal life mission. It's the process that determines how you will accomplish the mission that you've established for your life.

The Organizational Strategy

Organizational strategy or congregational strategy (if your ministry is a church) is what this book is all about. Again, the organizational strategy is a mission strategy. It's the strategy that you have designed to accomplish your ministry mission. Therefore, it's the broad, umbrella strategy that all the other strategies in your ministry will fit under. All the other strategies must come under the organizational strategy and aid it in some way in accomplishing the ministry's mission and vision.

The Departmental Strategy

I use the word *departmental* to include all the other strategies that exist in your ministry. Most organizations include ministries that fall under various departments or ministry areas. For example, a church may have a number of ministries such as Christian education, evangelism, worship, discipleship, small groups, and others. I argue in chapter 4 that each of these should have its own mission statement that falls within the parameters of the ministry's mission statement. Each must know what it's supposed to be doing or where it's going. For each department to accomplish its individual mission of evangelism, worship, and so forth, it must have its own unique strategy. Each must decide how it will lead people to worship, discipleship, and Christ. These are all ministrategies that fit within the mission strategy. If you cannot fit a departmental or ministry strategy under the mission strategy, then you must abandon it.

Questions for Thought and Discussion

1. A ministry may or may not have a mission statement. Does your ministry have one? If no, why not? Did it have one in the past? If yes, what was it? What happened to it? How will you develop a strategy without a mission?
2. Every ministry has a strategy. What is yours? Is it a good strategy? How do you know? Does it move people from prebirth to maturity? If no, why not? If yes, how?
3. Is it time to rethink your strategy? If you answered yes, then how do you know?
4. Do you have a personal ministry mission? If no, why not? If yes, have you developed a strategy to implement your personal mission? If no, why not?
5. Do the different departments or areas within your ministry have mission statements? If yes, do they have a strategy? Can they have a strategy without a mission? Explain.

Notes

1. I would recommend Guy Scaffold, *Strategic Planning for Christian Organizations* (Fayetteville, Ark.: Accrediting Association of Bible Colleges, 1994). This book deals more with planning for Christian schools, colleges, and seminaries, rather than churches.

2. Peter Drucker, *Managing the Non-Profit Organization* (New York: Harper Collins, 1990), 59.
3. Bob Gilliam, "Are Most Churches Intentionally Making Disciples?" Findings from the "Spiritual Journey Evaluation" (March 29, 1995), 1.
4. James F. Engel and H. Wilbert Norton, *What's Gone Wrong with the Harvest?* (Grand Rapids: Zondervan, 1975), 45.

10

The Development of a Strategy
How to Craft Your Strategy

With a clear definition of strategy in hand, Pastor Andy was ready to draft a strategy for Lake Country Church. Unlike the development of a vision, he would need the board's help. Like the development of a vision, the strategy, too, wouldn't come overnight. They would need some time.

Pastor Andy was excited about the prospect of working with his board on this vital project. Their relationship had changed appreciably. God had answered his prayers that he and the board would work together as a ministry team for the cause of Christ. He also sensed that through the discovery and development of the church's values, mission, vision, and now the strategy the board had accepted him as their shepherd and leader. They were comfortable with and confident in his leadership. Even Harry Smith appeared to have climbed aboard the ministry ship. God had used several older members of the board to help Harry rethink some of his ideas about how the church should be led.

Andy sensed that this church was about to go somewhere. Although they were at the bottom and looking up at the ministry hill, they were poised and prepared by God to take that hill for Christ. Their values and mission were Christ-honoring. The board affirmed them and communicated a sense of optimism that had eroded many years ago. Now they needed to come up with a significant, well-designed strategy to take them to the top of that hill.

Pastor Andy was aware of several excellent mission strategies that God has used in some other well-known churches across North America and abroad. The book he and the board were reading had warned against simply adopting one of those strategies. The reason? Lake Country wasn't one of those churches, Andy wasn't one of those churches' pastor, and Lake

Country ministered to different people in a different part of North America. What the book recommended was that Andy lead the board through a strategy-development process that would result in a strategy product that was true and endemic to Lake County Church. While they could learn much from those other strategies, they were not to mimic those strategies. The church needed a fresh strategy that was "homegrown."

This chapter is for leaders such as Pastor Andy who desire to craft a mission strategy that's not endemic to some other part of the world or North America but is their own. First, I will take you through the process of strategy development. Then I will provide a number of products as examples of what a good ministry strategy looks like.

The Process of Crafting Your Strategy

There are no less than six steps that you should take to develop a strategy for your church or parachurch ministry. I present them here and provide a summary of these steps at the end of this section.

Articulate the Mission Statement

The first step is to articulate your mission statement. Because both the vision and the strategy work off the mission statement, the strategy must begin with the mission statement clearly in mind. Again, you must know the "what" (mission) before you can develop the "how" (strategy). The tractor comes before the trailer. If up to this point you haven't drafted a complete, succinct mission statement, then you aren't ready to develop a strategy. It's not possible to charge the hill until you know what hill it is that you want to capture. You could capture the wrong hill!

Make certain that the board and other key leaders in the ministry understand and have ownership of the mission. You don't want to charge the hill under enemy fire only to discover as you arrive at the top that the rest of your troops are still bivouacked at the bottom of the hill. It would be a mistake to "go it alone." Strategy crafting is a team process that should result in a team product. You must arrive at the top of the hill with your team intact.

Divide the Mission Statement into Strategic Goals

The second step is to break the mission statement into specific strategic goals. The mission statement is the overarching goal of the ministry. Divide this overall goal into at least two major strategic goals and not more than five or six. It's possible that you might have more than six major goals but the strategy risks becoming unwieldy at that point. Look for some kind of natural, logical, or temporal progression that might help you put some kind of order to your major goals.

If your ministry is a local church, then your general mission is to make disciples (Matt. 28:19–20). Disciple making is a process. As you learned in chapter 9, it's the process of God's moving people from prebirth to maturity. The second step teaches you to break this process up into major strategic goals and look for some progression that will help you to order them. Some strategic goals are becoming, growing, serving, and making disciples. There is a logical, temporal progression to this process. Before you can grow, you have to be or become a disciple. This is conversion. Before you can serve Christ in your church, you should be a growing disciple. (Be cautious of placing new Christians in key ministry positions too quickly.) Before you can make disciples, you should be a serving disciple.

The mission (overall goal) of our church is to make disciples (Matt. 28:19–20). The strategic goals for making disciples are depicted in chart 10.1:

Goal #1:	To interest in becoming disciples
Goal #2:	To become growing disciples
Goal #3:	To become serving disciples
Goal #4:	To become disciple makers

Chart 10.1: Mission Goals

Envision Your Mission Statement

The third step is to envision the mission statement. This seems to be a simple statement of how you expand and develop the vision for your ministry as found in chapter 8. That is not what you're attempting here. This step is more focused than that of drafting a vision statement. If your ministry is a church, for example, you may choose a mission statement such as the following:

Our mission is to transform unchurched people into fully functioning followers of Christ.

The question is: What does a fully functioning follower of Christ look like? How would you know one if you met him or her?

To develop a fully functioning follower of Christ, you will need to develop a theology of discipleship. Out of a theology of discipleship will develop a set of specific, behavioral traits of a disciple. This approach will help you to know precisely what you're aiming at. It will also help you to communicate to the lay people in your ministry what a disciple is. To develop a set of observable, behavior traits you need to have a biblical view of discipleship. What does the Bible say that a disciple is? Study the gospels and Acts to see how the word *disciple* is used. Other terms, such as *follow* and to *come after* also speak of discipleship. Study passages from the epistles that concern the topic. Some characteristics of committed disciples are that:

- they deny themselves, take up their crosses, and follow Christ. In other words, they are willing to lose their lives for Christ's sake (Matt. 16:24–27; Mark 8:34–38; Luke 9:23–26; Acts 2:45; 4:32–35).
- they put Christ ahead of their families or love Christ more than their families. Scripture says that they must hate their own fathers and mothers, spouses and children, brothers and sisters, even their own lives (carrying your own cross) (Matt. 10:37; Luke 14:25–35). The use of the word *hate* here is problematic in North American culture. The word is a Semitic figure of speech or way of speaking that means to love less. The idea is that they must love and commit to Jesus more than to their families.
- they abide in Christ's word or follow his teachings (John 8:31; Acts 2:42).
- they love other disciples as Christ loves them (John 13:34–35; 15:11–17; Acts 2:42; 4:32).
- they bear fruit (John 15:7–17).
- they have been baptized (Matt. 28:19).
- they are obedient to Christ's commands (Matt. 28:20; John 15:9–10).

After you've discovered the behavioral traits of a Christ follower, you must determine how best to communicate these traits to your people. Chart 10.2 is an example of how to do this:

Trait #1:	They have a growing knowledge of the Bible and basic theology and are intentionally applying it to their lives (they are "hearers and doers" of the Word).
Trait #2:	They spend regular devotional time (worship, prayer, and Bible study) with God and instill this value in their families.
Trait #3:	They are regular attendees of church and actively participate in a small group.
Trait #4:	They understand their divine designs and are involved in one or more area(s) of ministry according to their gifts and abilities.
Trait #5:	They are building relationships with the lost, sharing Christ, and inviting them to a service relevant to them.
Trait #6:	They are generous, joyful givers of their God-given resources (time, talents, and treasure).

Chart 10.2: Traits of a Follower of Christ

There are also other good ways to communicate the characteristics of a disciple. One is found in the membership process of Willow Creek Community Church. It is called the Five-G process. According to Lynne Hybels, "it provides a forum for discussing and evaluating an individual's progress along the path of discipleship."[1] The five Gs are: grace, growth, group, gifts, and good stewardship. This is a very memorable approach to helping your people to know and remember the characteristics of discipleship. Perhaps you could use a four *s* process: salvation, sanctification, service, and stewardship; or a three *c* process: conversion, commitment, community.

Determine the Number of Steps to Accomplish the Mission

The fourth step is to determine the number of steps or stages that are necessary to accomplish the mission. If your ministry is a church, and the mission is to make disciples, you'll need to determine the number of steps it takes to make a disciple with the above traits. You may want to use some other word besides *steps*, such as *levels*, or *stages*. Regardless of the word you use, these steps will provide you with a structure or skeleton upon which you may drape or hang your strategy. Determining the number of steps is twofold. It involves (1) deciding the precise number of steps you will have in the process, and (2) identifying each.

Deciding the number of steps. It's very simple to determine the number of steps. They will be the same as the number of major strategic goals you discovered in step 2. You'll see why in the next strategy-development step. Most believe that Jesus' process for making disciples consisted of three to four steps. In *The Training of the Twelve*, A. B. Bruce sees three steps. Bill Hull in the *Disciple Making Pastor*, believes that Christ took his disciples through four steps or phases: "come and see," "come and follow me," "come and be with me," and "you will remain in me."[2] Willow Creek Community Church has developed a seven-step process for making disciples. There is no biblical imperative on the number of phases or steps that are necessary for making disciples or soul winners or anything else. Therefore, God gives each church the liberty to decide this matter for themselves.

Identifying the steps. You also need to identify each step or stage. At this point you'll need to determine what term you want to use whether it's *step*, *level*, *phase*, or something else. I encourage you to be creative and succinct. Figure 10.1 is one example that uses levels instead of steps:

Level 1: Investigating Christ
Level 2: Growing in Christ
Level 3: Ministering in Christ
Level 4: Leading in Christ

Figure 10.1: Levels Toward Accomplishing the Mission

Add a little creativity and you may come up with some steps that communicate memorably to your people. You might depict these levels as baseball bases (see figure 10.2), the ingredients of an apple (see figure 10.3), the layers of an onion, various battles in a war (to depict spiritual warfare) as in figure 10.4, or use stair steps (see figure 10.5). The following are examples:

> 1st Base: To inquire about becoming a disciple
> 2nd Base: To become a growing disciple
> 3rd Base: To become a serving disciple
> Home Plate: To become a disciple maker

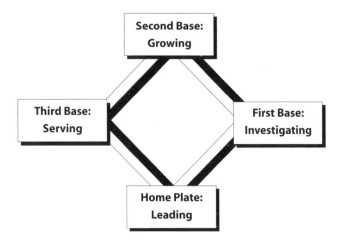

Figure 10.2: Baseball Diagram

> The Skin: Attracting Others to Christ
> The Meat: Growing and Ministering in Christ
> The Core: Leading in Christ

Figure 10.3: An Apple Diagram

Battle #1: To become Christ's warrior (enlisting)
Battle #2: To become a growing warrior (boot camp)
Battle #3: To become a serving warrior (active duty)
Battle #4: To become a warrior trainer (war college)

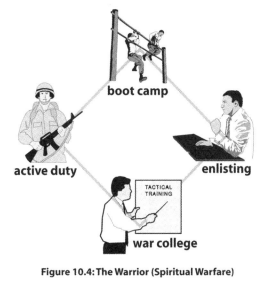

Figure 10.4: The Warrior (Spiritual Warfare)

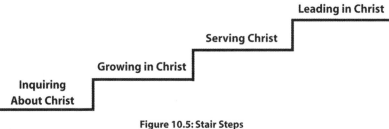

Figure 10.5: Stair Steps

Match Each Step with Its Goal

The fifth step is to match each step, level, or stage with its strategic goal. As I said in the prior step, each level will have its corresponding goal, and you determined these major strategic goals in step 2 above. Then place the appropriate goal under each step or level. Make sure the steps and their goals are sequential so that there is a logical or chronological flow. This is important because one will often build on another; thus providing a sense of spiritual movement or momentum for your people. People need to sense that they're growing and making progress in the faith. I have also provided a sample strategy in appendix G in the back of this book. Chart 10.3 is an example:

Level 1:	Interesting people in Christ
Goal:	To lead people to Christ and active involvement in the ministry.

Level 2:	Growing in Christ
Goal:	To grow people to spiritual maturity

Level 3:	Serving in Christ
Goal:	To equip people and involve people in ministry

Level 4:	Leading in Christ
Goal:	To enlist people for leadership at home and abroad

Chart 10.3: Steps Matched to Goals

Develop a Strategic Action for Each Strategic Goal

The sixth and final step is to develop a strategic action that will lead to each strategic goal. Every major goal must have a corresponding action that implements it. Other words for action are *method*, *vehicle*, or *objective*. Developing a strategic action for each goal involves thinking through several areas such as the strategy's source, traits, age groups, time, and even a diagram that communicates the strategy.

The source. Much of the information that makes up your strategy comes from your answer to the question: What kind of church will it take to reach our target group? The answer focuses on things such as the kind of meetings, worship, teaching, evangelism, and so on that you will implement in your church. The sample strategy document in appendix G shows the effect of the various sources on the strategy.

The behavioral traits. In designing your strategy, you will need to take into account the behavioral traits of a disciple that you list as the result of taking the third step above. Here is where you place that information. Ask: How and where does the strategy accomplish each trait? A helpful check is to note in parenthesis after the strategy statement which trait the strategy accomplishes. I suggest that you put the trait in bold type for quick recognition as I have done in the sample in appendix G.

Age groups. You must also consider how you plan to disciple the various age groups in your church. A part of our mission is to disciple all of our people, including young people. Will you have an age-graded Sunday school program or a learning center? Will the children, teens, and adults be in small groups? Will young people have their own large group meetings?

Time. Determine approximately how much time you think it will take to accomplish each level or step. In other words, how long should it take or will it take to move someone through each level? What is a reasonable time span for each? What should your expectations and their expectations be so that both of you can judge the progress. Lee Strobel, one of the pastors at Willow Creek Community Church, states that he spent two years as a seeker before coming to faith in Christ. Is two years too short, too long, or typical for a seeker in your community? What should you expect?

Diagram. Devise a diagram that communicates the entire strategy (all the levels of commitment) to your people. This will help them to easily remember the strategy. In addition, they will know where they have been and where they need to go in their growth toward Christlikeness. The former is a source of encouragement. The latter provides a challenge. I have already suggested this above for each level. It's important that you come up with creative ways to communicate all the levels of commitment or steps of discipleship to your people. Some examples from above are the baseball bases, an apple, concentric circles, the layers of an onion, spiritual battles to be fought and won, as well as others.

A summary of the strategy process is found in chart 10.4.

1.	Articulate the mission statement (overall goal)
2.	Divide the mission statement into strategic goals
3.	Envision the mission statement
4.	Determine the steps to accomplish the mission
5.	Match each step with its strategic goal
6.	Develop a strategic action-step for each strategic goal

Chart 10.4: The Strategy Process

The Product of Crafting Your Strategy

Now that you have a process for drafting a strategy that is tailor-made for your ministry and the people in your part of the country, the next step is to move from the strategy process to the strategy product. This involves studying and learning from the work that others have done in developing a strategy for their ministries. The questions to ask are: How similar is their situation to ours? and, What in their strategies might prove helpful to ours? The following examples provide sample strategies.

Willow Creek Community Church

Willow Creek Community Church is located in a suburb of Chicago. Several church planters led by Bill Hybels started Willow Creek in 1975, and it has grown to be one of the largest churches in America. What is impressive is not so much its size but that the majority of its people have come to faith and maturity as the result of the ministry of this church. Carl George observes that most large ministries are receptor churches. They continue to grow not as the result of evangelism but because of people transferring from other small churches. Willow Creek has defied this trend and regularly updates its ministries and seeks to do whatever it takes within biblical means to accomplish God's purpose for its ministry.

Key to Willow Creek's growth and blessing is a clear, significant mission statement and strategy (see figure 10.6). The church is a new-paradigm ministry that has worked hard at crafting and redrafting a strategy that implements their biblical mission.

Mission. The mission of Willow Creek Community Church is to turn irreligious people into fully devoted followers of Jesus Christ. The following fourfold statement of purpose expands and explains this mission.

Exaltation: Willow Creek Community Church exists to offer the body of believers the opportunity to worship and glorify God together.

Edification: Willow Creek Community Church exists to help believers build a foundation of biblical understanding, establish a devotional life, discover their spiritual gifts, and to encourage believers to become participating members in the body of Christ.

Evangelism: Willow Creek Community Church exists to reach people who are facing a Christless eternity. Members of the body are encouraged to seek out the unchurched as the Holy Spirit has sought them out, and to look for opportunities to share Christ's love.

Social Action: Willow Creek Community Church exists to act as a conscience to the world by demonstrating the love and righteousness of God in both word and deed.

Strategy. Willow Creek Community Church has developed the following seven-step strategy to accomplish the above mission statement.

Bridge building: Every believer attending Willow Creek Community Church is strongly challenged to build a relationship of integrity with their unchurched friends. (Program: Uses an Evangelism Ministry team that offers seminars and classes.)

Sharing a verbal witness: Once a relationship of integrity has been established, believers will have an opportunity to share their testimonies with unchurched Harry or Mary, the church's target group. (Program: Same as bridge building.)

Providing a service for seekers: Most unchurched who hear about a believer's relationship with Christ will not immediately respond with a decision to establish a similar relationship. It is at this point that believers need a place to bring their unchurched friends so that they will continue to be challenged in a relevant creative and contemporary way to consider the claims of Christ. (Program: A seeker-sensitive service on the weekends designed to supplement the believer's evangelistic efforts.)

Attending the New Community service: Once someone has accepted Jesus as Savior and has been attending the weekend service for a time, he is encouraged to become involved in the midweek believer's service that provides believers with the opportunity to participate in corporate worship and to listen to expository teaching designed to mature the believer. This service is imperative for those who are committed to becoming fully devoted followers of Christ. (Program: A midweek service specifically for believers focusing on worship, in-depth Bible study, and prayer.)

Participating in a small group: Believers who are involved in New Community are encouraged to take the next step in their Christian walk by participating in a small group that provides fellowship for the believer as well as a group for accountability, discipleship, encouragement, and support. (Program: Small-group ministries.)

Involved in service: Believers who consider Willow Creek Community Church their home church are encouraged to discover their spiritual gift(s), develop them, and then use them in some form of Christian service within the body of Christ. (Program: The Network Ministry and its seminars help believers discover their divine designs and connect with ministry.)

Stewardship: Believers need to be educated in the area of money management and to recognize their individual responsibility to manage their money in a God-glorifying manner. It is important that every believer recognize that stewardship is a form of discipleship and that giving is a form of worship. (Program: Uses the Good Sense Ministry Team to conduct seminars on biblical

Willow Creek's 7-Step Philosophy of Ministry

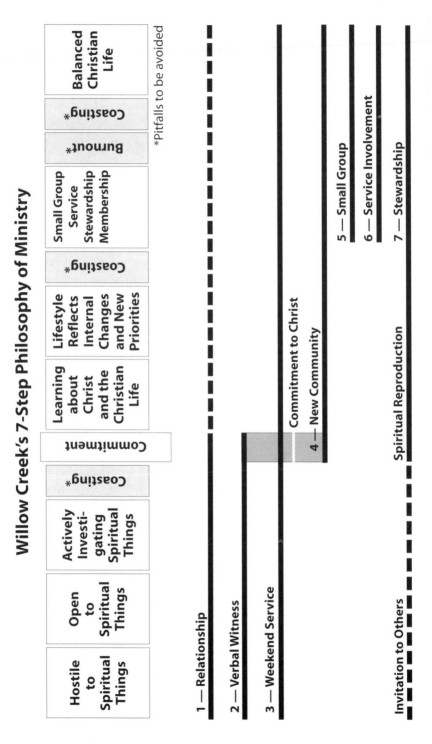

| Hostile to Spiritual Things | Open to Spiritual Things | Actively Investigating Spiritual Things | Coasting* | Commitment | Learning about Christ and the Christian Life | Lifestyle Reflects Internal Changes and New Priorities | Coasting* | Small Group Service Stewardship Membership | Burnout* | Coasting* | Balanced Christian Life |

*Pitfalls to be avoided

1 — Relationship

2 — Verbal Witness

3 — Weekend Service

Commitment to Christ

4 — New Community

5 — Small Group

6 — Service Involvement

7 — Stewardship

Spiritual Reproduction

Invitation to Others

Figure 10.6: Willow Creek's 7-Step Philosophy of Ministry

foundations for money management. Also has a team of trained budget counselors for family budget counseling.)

Saddleback Valley Community Church

Rick Warren is the founding pastor of Saddleback Valley Community Church, a Southern Baptist ministry, located in Mission Viejo, California. The church began in 1980 with just two families and has since grown to between eight and ten thousand people in attendance. Rick's passion is to reach the unchurched of his community with the Gospel of Christ and see them grow to maturity (see figure 10.7). Consequently, approximately 70 percent of the membership has accepted the Savior through the witness of this church. Saddleback has also sponsored fifteen daughter churches in the time that Rick has been its pastor.

Mission. The mission of Saddleback Valley Community Church is to bring people to Jesus and *membership* in his family, develop them to Christlike *maturity*, and equip them for *ministry* in the church and life *mission* in the world, in order to *magnify* God's name.

The following fivefold statement of purpose serves to further clarify this mission statement. Saddleback Community Church exists to celebrate God's presence in worship (magnify), to communicate God's Word through evangelism (mission), to incorporate God's family into our fellowship (membership), to educate God's people through discipleship (maturity), and to demonstrate God's love through service (ministry).

Strategy. Saddleback's strategy consists of five levels of commitment. They desire to move people from the first which is community (unchurched lost people) to the last which is the core (the dedicated minority of workers and leaders).

Evangelism: To have impact on the community—the pool of lost who live within driving distance of the church. (Use an annual series of community-wide Bridge Events: concerts, special services, and productions.)

Worship: To reach the crowd—the believers and unbelievers who attend one of the worship services every weekend. (Use the weekend seeker service.)

Fellowship: To move the crowd into the congregation—the church's official members. (Use Class 101 and a small-group network.)

Discipleship: To move the congregation to commitment—people who are serious about their faith but aren't actively serving a church ministry. (Use the midweek service and the Life

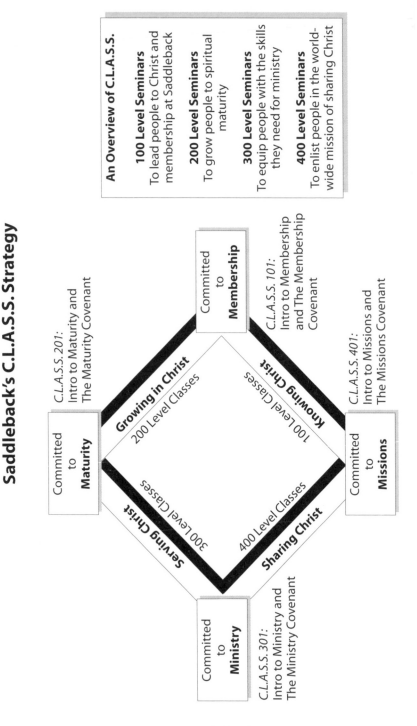

Saddleback's C.L.A.S.S. Strategy

An Overview of C.L.A.S.S.

100 Level Seminars
To lead people to Christ and membership at Saddleback

200 Level Seminars
To grow people to spiritual maturity

300 Level Seminars
To equip people with the skills they need for ministry

400 Level Seminars
To enlist people in the world-wide mission of sharing Christ

Committed to **Membership**

C.L.A.S.S. 101:
Intro to Membership and The Membership Covenant

C.L.A.S.S. 201:
Intro to Maturity and The Maturity Covenant

Committed to **Maturity**

Growing in Christ
200 Level Classes

Knowing Christ
100 Level Classes

Serving Christ
300 Level Classes

Sharing Christ
400 Level Classes

Committed to **Missions**

C.L.A.S.S. 401:
Intro to Missions and The Missions Covenant

Committed to **Ministry**

C.L.A.S.S. 301:
Intro to Ministry and The Ministry Covenant

Figure 10.7: Saddleback's C.L.A.S.S. Strategy

Development Institute: Bible studies, seminars [Class 201], workshops, independent study programs, and so on.)

Ministry: To bring the committed into the core—the dedicated minority of workers and leaders. (Use the monthly S.A.L.T. [Saddleback Advanced Leadership Training] meeting and Class 301.)

Pantego Bible Church

Pantego Bible Church, a part of the Bible church movement that flourished in the days following World War II, is located in Arlington, Texas, between Dallas and Fort Worth. Its first pastor spent twenty-five years with the church and led it to significant growth. In the mid to late 1970s, however, a crisis developed that resulted in significant decline. The worship attendance plummeted from 1,300 to 425 and contributions to the general fund went from $16,000 a week to $4,000 a week.

In February of 1990, Randy Frazee became the senior pastor and implemented a mission and strategy that has led the church out of its malaise (see figure 10.8). It is targeting the unchurched that make up 74 percent of the 270,000 Arlington residents. In just four years, the worship attendance has climbed from 425 to more than 1,200 and the offerings have increased at a rate of 20 to 25 percent each year.

Mission. The mission of Pantego Bible Church is to transform people, through the work of the Holy Spirit, into fully developing followers of Christ.

Strategy. The strategy consists of four stages based on Acts 2:42–47 (teaching, fellowship, the breaking of bread, and prayer).

Stage One: Establishing a relationship with God (a believer).
Stage Two: Putting God at the center of my life (a worshiping believer).
Stage Three: Applying God's principles to my life (a growing believer).
Stage Four: Making an impact with my life (a serving believer).

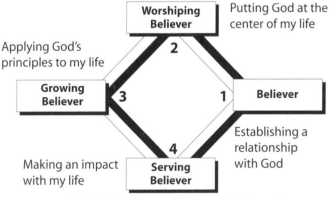

Figure 10.8: The Pantego Bible Church Diamond

The Evangelical Free Church

The Evangelical Free Church has adopted the T-Net Program that is based on Bill Hull's book, *The Disciple Making Pastor*.[3] Bill Hull, Bob Gilliam, and others are conducting seminars around the country at which they are sharing disciple-making principles not only with Evangelical Free churches but any who are interested in reaching their world for Christ. They provide the following mission and strategy.

Mission. The church's mission is to make every willing person a healthy, reproducing believer.

Strategy. The strategy consists of four phases.

Phase 1: "Come and See."
Objective: To introduce to Christ and his work.
Vehicles: Sunday morning worship service, the minicongregation (small groups), and Velcro ministries (choirs, sports teams, men's clubs, children's activities, and so forth).

Phase 2: "Come and Follow Me."
Objective: To train and establish people as mature disciples.
Vehicle: Training in the Word of God, prayer, fellowship (relationships), and witnessing (outreach) in the context of a discipleship small group.

Phase 3: "Come and Be with Me."
Objective: To select and train leadership.
Vehicles: The classroom (learn six ministry skills) and on-the-job training (leading a small group, labor team, and so forth).

Phase 4: "Remain in Me."
Objective: To deploy professional leaders in professional ministries and lay leaders in local ministries.
Vehicles: Professional leaders will plant churches, pastor churches, and become missionaries. Lay leaders will serve as elders, deacons, and so forth.

Equipping the Saints

God has raised up various parachurch organizations such as the Navigators, Campus Crusade for Christ, and Equipping the Saints to focus on areas where the church has proved weak such as in evangelism and discipleship. These ministries could teach the church much about discipleship because they are out making disciples. Therefore, it is well worth the leader's time to obtain their materials and investigate what they are doing and how they are doing it.

David Dawson was the national director for the Navigators in the nation of Singapore when he developed Equipping the Saints (ETS).[4] It is a parachurch ministry designed to help churches and mission agencies train lay people to make disciples. The initial challenge was to train people in the local church as effectively as they had through the parachurch or Navigators. This meant that David would have to condense what was normally anywhere from two to five years of training into a shorter time—at the most three to six weeks. Dawson developed the ETS program over a six year involvement with a group of Singapore churches. During this time, it also underwent extensive field testing.

The ETS program is heavily into Bible study and Scripture memorization. It's organized around the following major subject areas:

1. The Layman and the Great Commission
2. Personal and Spiritual Management
3. Evangelism
4. Basic Christian Living
5. Follow-up
6. Discipleship
7. Advanced Follow-up
8. Leadership
9. Christian Character
10. Visual Survey of the Bible

Under each subject area various topics are covered to develop that subject. For example, the program breaks the topic of discipleship into the following:

1. Definition of Discipleship
2. A Principle of Discipleship
3. The Focal Point of Discipleship
4. Commitment to Discipleship
5. Finding the Will of God
6. Spiritual Reproduction
7. Interpersonal relationships

Questions for Thought and Discussion

1. Have you developed a ministry mission statement? If no, why not? If yes, can you break down the mission into several major goals? What are they? Do you see a logical or temporal flow to them?
2. When you envision the mission statement what do you see? If your ministry is a church, what do you see? Do you see a disciple or

Christ follower? Have you developed a theology of discipleship? What are the traits of a completely committed disciple?

3. How many steps would your strategy have? (Count the number of strategic goals from question 1.) Will you call them *steps* or do you plan to use some other term? In identifying your steps, did you find yourself attracted to one of the models that attempts to communicate creatively the strategy to your people? If not, have you come up with a creative one of your own?

4. Match each step with its strategic goal. Is there a logical or temporal flow? Will they provide a sense of spiritual movement or momentum?

5. Developing a strategic action will take some time. Any thoughts at this point about what kind of things that you would like to see in these actions?

6. Do you find the sample strategy statements from the various ministry organizations helpful in crafting a strategy? Is so, how? Did you find that you were attracted to a particular one? Is so, which one? Any idea why?

7. Are you aware of any other disciple-making programs? If yes, what are they? How might they be helpful to you and your ministry?

Notes

1. Lynne Hybels and Bill Hybels, *Rediscovering Church* (Grand Rapids: Zondervan, 1995), 134.

2. Bill Hull, *The Disciple Making Pastor* (Old Tappen, N.J.: Revell, 1988), 214.

3. For further information about the T-Net program, write to the following address: EFCA, Training Network, 901 East 78th St., Minneapolis, MN 55420.

4. You may obtain information and material from the following: Equipping the Saints, 4400 Moulton Street, Suite D, Greenville, TX 75401. (903) 455-3782; fax (903) 454-8524.

Appendix A
Acadiana Community Church:
Credo and Doctrinal Statement*

Our Values

We Value Full Devotion to Christ and His Cause

We believe that whole-hearted devotion to Jesus Christ is not only the biblical norm for the believer, but that anything less is sin in God's eyes. Full devotion should be expected of and encouraged by every believer in the community.

We Value Being a Biblically Functioning Community

We believe that the first priority of any church is to be and do the things that God expects of a biblically functioning community, that is devotion to the Word, worship, and walk of God.

We Value Having a Great Commission Vision

We believe that if we are to be the church we must have God's vision for the church, which is ultimately to glorify the Father by continuing Christ's earthly ministry of seeking, saving, and serving. We do this when we make disciples by reaching and teaching the unchurched to be fully devoted followers of Jesus Christ.

We Value Culturally Adapting Ministry

We believe that while the truth of God's Word never changes, the culture in which we are called to apply these unchanging principles of truth is ever changing. Therefore, we must understand our culture and

---

* Used by permission.

minister the truth of God's Word in the most effective way possible, even if this means laying aside some of the man-made traditions of the church.

We Value Lost People as God Values Lost People

We believe that lost people are valuable to God and therefore should be equally valuable to us. We spend time and energy on that which we value, therefore, we should spend time and energy pursuing lost people as Christ did when He was on this earth.

We Value Biblical Culturally Relevant Evangelism

We believe that evangelism begins with our willingness to befriend and build relationships with lost people. We also believe that it is the work of the Spirit of God to bring people into His kingdom. Our responsibility is to be faithful in showing God's love to the lost through caring relationships and to be ready to share the gospel with them through a variety of methods as the Holy Spirit gives opportunity.

We Value Authentic Holistic Worship

We believe that man was made to worship God and that a primary responsibility of the individual and church corporately is to worship God in spirit and truth. We believe this worship should involve the whole person: body, emotions, intellect, and will. We also believe this worship is a lifestyle of obedience, not simply a once a week experience.

We Value Equipping and Mobilizing Members to Minister

We believe that everyone in the body of Christ has been uniquely designed to serve God. This Divine Design involves personality, spiritual giftedness, experience, and passion. We believe that it is the responsibility of the church corporately to equip, encourage, and actively help the individual believer find the place where God has designed him or her to serve in the body of Christ. We understand that this place of service may or may not be within the traditional programs of the church.

We Value Strong Servant Leadership

We believe that Christ is ultimately the only head of the church, but that He has chosen to function through human leaders in the local church. We believe that these human leaders must meet the biblical qualifications of leadership. They must have godly character, biblical vision, and influence. We believer leadership must be team leadership if it is to be biblical and effective in our culture. But we also realize that, as with all biblical teams, this team leadership must be led by a visionary leader of leaders. Leadership must model the leadership of Christ in that it is both strong leadership and servant leadership. Hence, we believe that the church should be led by strong servant team leadership led by a strong servant leader of leaders.

Doctrinal Statement

The Bible

We believe that the original manuscripts of the Old and New Testament comprise the full, word-for-word, truthful, inerrant Word of God which is the supreme and final authority in doctrine and practice. (Isa. 40:8; 2 Tim. 3:16–17; Heb. 4:12; 2 Peter 1:20–21)

The Trinity

We believe in one God eternally existing in three equal persons— Father, Son, and Holy Spirit, who have the same nature and attributes but who are distinct in office and activity. (Deut. 6:4; Isa. 48:16; Jer. 10:10; Matt. 28:19; John 10:30; Acts 5:3–4; 2 Cor. 13:14; Heb. 1:8)

The Father

We believe that as eternal Father, He is the Father of all men in the non-salvation, Creator-creature sense, the Father of the nation Israel, the Father of the Lord Jesus Christ, and the spiritual Father of all who believe in Christ. He is the author of salvation, the One who sent the Son, and the disciplinarian of His children. (Exod. 4:22; Ps. 2:7–9; John 5:37; Acts 17:29; Gal. 3:26; Eph. 1:3–6; Heb. 12:9; 1 Peter 1:3)

The Person and Work of Jesus Christ

We believe Jesus Christ is God incarnate, conceived by the Holy Spirit, born of a virgin, completely God and completely man. We believe in His pre-existence, His sinless life, His substitutionary atonement, His bodily resurrection from the grave, His ascension into heaven, and His bodily return from heaven. (John 1:1, 14, 18; Luke 1:35; Rom. 3:24–26; 4:25; 1 Peter 1:3–5; Eph. 4:11–16; 1 Thess. 4:13–18; Heb. 1:3; 7:23–25; 1 John 2:1–2)

The Holy Spirit

We believe that the Holy Spirit regenerates, indwells, baptizes, seals, and bestows spiritual gifts upon all believers at the time of their conversion. Experientially, He fills, teaches, leads, assures, and prays for believers. (John 14:26; 16:6–15; Acts 1:5; 2:1–4; 11:1–18; Rom. 8:14–16, 26–27; 1 Cor. 6:19; 12:7–11, 13; Eph. 1:13–14; 5:18; 2 Thess. 2:1–10; Titus 3:5)

Man and Sin

We believe man was created in the image of God; that he sinned in Adam and thereby incurred both physical and spiritual death (separation from God); is now a sinner, by nature and by choice; and is in need of salvation. (Gen. 1:1, 27; 2:17; 3:1–19; Isa. 14:12–14; Luke 20:36; Heb. 1:13–14; 2:5–8; 1 Peter 2:4; Jude 6; John 12:31; Heb. 2:14; Rev. 20:10; John 1:1–3; 8:44; Col. 1:16–17; Rom. 5:12–21; Eph. 2:1–3)

Salvation

We believe in salvation by grace through faith in Jesus Christ's substitutionary payment for our sins, not based on human merit, works, or religious ceremony. We believe that anyone who has placed their faith in Christ is eternally secure, has everlasting life, will not come into condemnation, and shall never perish. We believe that assurance comes to the believer from three primary sources: trusting the Word of God's promises, the witness of the Holy Spirit, and a persevering walk with the Lord. (John 1:12; 2:3, 16; 2 Cor. 5:17–21; Eph. 2:8–9; Titus 3:4–7; Dan. 12:1–2; Matt. 25:31–46; John 3:16, 36; 5:24; 10:28–29; 11:25–26; Rom. 8:28–39; 1 John 4:11–13; Jude 1; Rev. 20:12–15)

The Church

We believe in the church, both universally and locally, as the spiritual body of which Christ is the Head, and in the practices of water baptism of believers and the Lord's Supper as the ordinances of the local church. (Matt. 16:18; Acts 1:5; 11:15; 1 Cor. 12:13; Eph. 1:22–23; 4:11–16; 5:22–33; Col. 1:18)

The Great Commission

We believe that those whom God has saved are sent into the world by Christ as He was by the Father. Those so sent are ambassadors, commissioned to go make disciples and make Christ known to the whole world. We also believe that everyone should have an opportunity to carefully examine the facts about Christ and have a chance to make an intelligent decision about Him. (Matt. 28:18–20; John 15:17–18, 20-21; Acts 1; Rom. 10:14–15; 2 Cor. 5:18–20; Col. 4:2–6; 2 Tim. 2:14–26)

Eternity

We believe in the physical resurrection of the human body (at the second coming of Christ); in the eternal conscious existence of all individuals in either heaven or hell; and in the rewards of the saved and the punishment of the lost for eternity. (1 Cor. 15; Luke 16:19–31; 2 Cor. 5:8–10; 1 Cor. 3:11–15)

Appendix B
Church Credos*

The Jerusalem Church, Jerusalem, Israel

Core Values

1. We value expository teaching (Acts 2:42–43).
2. We value fellowship (Acts 2:42).
3. We value prayer (Acts 2:42).
4. We value biblical community (Acts 2:44–46).
5. We value praise and worship (Acts 2:47).
6. We value evangelism (Acts 2:47).

Fellowship Bible Church, Dallas, Texas

We have ten core values that guide us. These values describe the culture that we seek to create at FBC. We aspire to be:

1. Biblically Faithful: We make Scripture the final authority rather than church tradition. We seek to be innovative and flexible as long as we do not violate Scripture.
2. Culturally Relevant: We try to adapt our ministry to current needs and trends in American life, without compromising biblical absolutes. We attempt to communicate the good news of Jesus Christ to American society in ways it can understand.
3. Grace Oriented: We emphasize God's unconditional acceptance and full forgiveness through Jesus Christ. We attempt to motivate people through love and thankfulness rather than guilt, shame, and duty.
4. Seeker Sensitive: We know that many who are not yet committed

* Used by permission.

to Christ are attracted to our ministry; therefore, we desire to create a non-threatening environment in which they are free to explore the Christian faith at their own pace.

5. Growth Responsive: We appreciate the advantages of a small, intimate congregation, but also feel we should respond to the numerical growth that often results from reaching out to those who are exploring Christianity. We do not set a particular limit on the size of our congregation, but trust God to show the church leadership what our facilities should be and how best to utilize them.

6. Relationally Centered: We stress healthy relationships among Christians. We emphasize small groups as a primary means for Christians to care for each other, develop friendships, and share their lives.

7. People Developing: We seek to help people grow spiritually. We provide biblical instruction, and we encourage believers to discover and exercise their spiritual gifts.

8. Family Affirming: We seek to provide an atmosphere which strengthens marriages and families. We are committed to strong youth and children's programs.

9. Simply Structured: We assign the ultimate leadership of the church to elders and the daily operations of the church to paid staff who are responsible to set up effective programs.

10. Cross Culturally Effective: We reach beyond our own culture as we seek to have an effective impact on others cultures with the gospel.

Lakeview Community Church, Cedar Hill, Texas

This statement of principles clarifies the attitudes and approaches that will be encouraged in the ministries of Lakeview Community Church. Most of these are not biblical absolutes, but they represent our understanding of how to most effectively accomplish our purpose.

1. A Commitment to Relevant Bible Exposition
   We believe that the Bible is God's inspired Word, the authoritative and trustworthy rule of faith and practice for Christians. The Bible is both timeless and timely, relevant to the common needs of all people at all times and to the specific problems of contemporary living. Therefore, we are committed to equipping Christians, through the preaching and teaching of God's Word, to follow Christ in every sphere of life.

2. A Commitment to Prayer
   We believe that God desires his people to pray and that he hears and answers prayer (Matt. 7:7–11; James 5:13–18). Therefore, the ministries and activities of this church will be characterized

by a reliance on prayer in their conception, planning, and execution.

3. A Commitment to Lay Ministry

We believe that the primary responsibility of the pastor(s) and teachers in the local church is to "prepare God's people for works of service" (Eph. 4:12). Therefore, the ministry of Lakeview Community Church will be placed as much as possible in the hands of nonvocational workers. This will be accomplished through training opportunities and through practices which encourage lay initiation, leadership, responsibility, and authority in the various ministries of the church.

4. A Commitment to Small Groups

We are committed to small-group ministry as one of the most effective means of building relationships, stimulating spiritual growth, and developing leaders.

5. An Appreciation for Creativity and Innovation

In today's rapidly changing world, forms and methods must be continually evaluated, and if necessary, altered to fit new conditions. While proven techniques should not be discarded at a whim, we encourage creativity and innovation, flexibility and adaptability. We are more concerned with effectiveness in ministry than with adherence to tradition.

6. A Commitment to Excellence

We believe that the God of our salvation deserves the best we have to offer. The Lord himself is a God of excellence, as shown by the beauty of creation; further, he gave the best that he had, his only Son, for us (Rom. 8:32). Paul exhorts servants, in whatever they do, to "work at it with all your heart, as working for the Lord, not for men" (Col. 3:23). Therefore, in the ministries and activities of Lakeview Community Church we will seek to maintain a high standard of excellence to the glory of God. This will be achieved when every person is exercising his or her God-given spiritual gift to the best of his or her ability (1 Cor. 12).

7. A Commitment to Growth

Although numerical growth is not necessarily a sign of God's blessing, and is not a sufficient goal in itself, we believe that God desires for us to reach as many people as possible with the life-changing message of Jesus Christ. Therefore, we will pursue methods and policies which will facilitate numerical growth, without compromising in any way our integrity or our commitment to biblical truth.

Saddleback Valley Community Church, Mission Viejo, California

Our Statement of Values

We are a purpose-drive, value-based church.

1. We Value the Application of Scripture
   "Do not merely listen to the word, and so deceive yourselves. Do what it says" (James 1:22).
2. We Value Service
   "Your attitude must be like my own, for I did not come to be served, but to serve" (Matt. 20:28 TLB).
   "David had served God's purpose in his own generation" (Acts 13:36).
   "Let love make you serve one another" (Gal. 5:13 GNB).
3. We Value Excellence
   "Each one should test his own actions. Then he can take pride in himself, without comparing himself to somebody else" (Gal. 6:4).
   "The quality of each person's work will be seen when the Day of Christ exposes it" (1 Cor. 3:13 GNB).
4. We Value Feedback
   "A fool thinks he needs no advice, but a wise man listens to others" (Prov. 12:15 TLB)
   "Get the facts at any price" (Prov. 23:23 TLB).
   "Every prudent man acts out of knowledge" (Prov. 13:16).
   "Be sure you know the condition of your flocks, give careful attention to your herds" (Prov. 27:23).
   "Reliable communication permits progress" (Prov. 13:17 TLB).
5. We Value Authenticity
   "Our lives in this world, and especially our relations with you, have been ruled by God-given frankness and sincerity" (2 Cor. 1:12 GNB).
   "We are hiding nothing from you and our hearts are absolutely open to you" (2 Cor. 6:11).
6. We Value Informality
   "A relaxed attitude lengthens a man's life" (Prov. 14:30 TLB).
7. We Value People's Giftedness
   "God has given each of us the ability to do certain things well" (Rom. 12:6 TLB)
   "Each one should use whatever gift he has received to serve others" (1 Peter 4:10).
8. We Value People's Differences
   "There are all sorts of services to be done, but always to the

same Lord; working in all sorts of different ways in different people" (1 Cor. 12:5 JB).

"Accept one another then, just as Christ has accepted you" (Rom. 15:7).

"Live together in harmony, live together in love, as though you have only one mind and one spirit between you" (Phil. 2:2).

9. We Value Continual Learning

"He who loves wisdom loves his own best interest and will be a success" (Prov. 19:8 TLB).

"If the ax is dull, and its edge unsharpened, more strength is needed but skill will bring success" (Eccles. 10:10).

10. We Value Simplicity

"God made us plain and simple but we have made ourselves very complicated" (Eccles. 7:29 GNB).

"When I came to you, it was not with any show of oratory or philosophy, but simply to tell you what God has guaranteed" (1 Cor. 2:1 JB).

11. We Value Teamwork

"Now you are the body of Christ, and each one of you is a part of it" (1 Cor. 12:27).

"Two are better off than one, because together they can work more effectively" (Eccles. 4:9 GNB).

"In Christ we who are many form one body, and each member belongs to all the others" (Rom. 12:5).

12. We Value Innovation

"The intelligent man is always open to new ideas. In fact, he looks for them" (Prov. 18:15 TLB).

13. We Value Freedom and Flexibility

"Where the Spirit of the Lord is, there is freedom" (2 Cor. 3:17).

"We may make our plans, but God has the last word" (Prov. 16:1 GNB).

14. We Value Humor

"Being cheerful keeps you healthy. It is a slow death to be gloomy all the time" (Prov. 17:22 GNB).

"God . . . richly provides us with everything for our enjoyment" (1 Tim. 6:17).

15. We Value Optimism

"All things are possible with God" (Mark 10:27).

"According to your faith will it be done to you" (Matt. 9:29).

16. We Value Growth

"Under Christ's control, the whole body is nourished and held together...and it grows as God wants it to grow" (Col. 2:19 GNB).

17. We Value Commitment

"First they gave themselves to the Lord; and then, by God's will they gave themselves to us as well" (2 Cor. 8:5 GNB).

Willow Creek Community Church, South Barrington, Illinois

1. We believe that anointed teaching is the catalyst for transformation in individuals' lives and in the church.

   This includes the concept of teaching for life change—Romans 12:7, 2 Timothy 3:16–17, James 1:23–25.

2. We believe that lost people matter to God, and therefore, ought to matter to the church.

   This includes the concepts of relational evangelism and evangelism as a process—Luke 5:30–32, Luke 15, Matthew 18:14.

3. We believe that the church should be culturally relevant while remaining doctrinally pure.

   This includes the concept of sensitively relating to our culture through our facility, printed materials, and use of the arts—1 Corinthians 9:19–23.

4. We believe that Christ-followers should manifest authenticity and yearn for continuous growth.

   This includes the concepts of personal authenticity, character, and wholeness—Ephesians 4:25–26, 32; Hebrews 12:1; Philippians 1:6.

5. We believe that a church should operate as a unified community of servants with men and women stewarding their spiritual gifts.

   This includes the concepts of unity, servanthood, spiritual gifts, and ministry calling—1 Corinthians 12 and 14, Romans 12, Ephesians 4, Psalm 133:1.

6. We believe that loving relationships should permeate every aspect of church life.

   This includes the concepts of love-driven ministry, ministry accomplished in teams and relationship building—1 Corinthians 13, Nehemiah 3, Luke 10:1, John 13:34–35.

7. We believe that life-change happens best in small groups.

   This includes the concepts of discipleship, vulnerability, and accountability—Luke 6:12–13, Acts 2:44–47.

8. We believe that excellence honors God and inspires people.

   This includes the concepts of evaluation, critical review, intensity and excellence—Colossians 3:17, Malachi 1:6–14, Proverbs 27:17.

9. We believe that churches should be led by men and women with leadership gifts.

   This includes the concepts of empowerment, servant leadership, strategic focus, and intentionality—Nehemiah 1–2, Romans 12:8, Acts 6:2–5.

10. We believe that the pursuit of full devotion to Christ and His cause is normal for every believer.

This includes the concepts of stewardship, servanthood, downward mobility, and the pursuit of kingdom goals—1 Kings 11:4, Philippians 2:1–11, 2 Corinthians 8:7.

Wooddale Church, Eden Prairie, Minnesota

Our Church Values

"The purpose of Wooddale Church is to honor God by making more disciples for Jesus Christ."

Values are what Wooddale Church lives by to fulfill our purpose.

God-Centered

Wooddale Church exists for God. In every person and program God is first, God is experienced and God is to be pleased. We delight to constantly have God on our minds and in our conversations. Wooddale Church is the people and place where God is experienced. Public gathering to worship is a primary expression. Personal godly living is an equally important expression.

Bible-Based

Wooddale Church lives by the Bible. Bible teaching permeates every program because we want to know and understand God's Word. The Bible must be lived out in our lives because we believe the Bible is God's Word for what we believe and do. Learning and living the Bible is natural and normal to Wooddale Church.

Outreach-Oriented

Wooddale Church looks outward to serve non-Christians and the unchurched in order to reach them for Jesus Christ. This is woven into everything we do. Outreach orientation requires awareness of our culture and connecting to people as they are and where they are. When a choice is made between serving needs on the inside or reaching out to others, we are committed in advance toward ministry to outsiders. This is done to fulfill our purpose to make more disciples for Jesus Christ.

Disciple Making

Christians are disciples—believers who are learning and changing to be more like Jesus. Disciple-making is happening when Wooddalers live Christianly, especially under stress, and especially in demonstrating

Christian love in relationships with others. Wooddale Church is a university for disciple-making—offering courses, networking relationships, providing community, showcasing examples, serving as a laboratory, and offering a context for continuous disciple-making.

We will continually change to get the job done. We will include classes, seminars, retreats, mentoring, counseling, and discipling. When appropriate, we will encourage Christians to take advantage of disciple-making opportunities at other churches or through outside organizations. We are far more interested in developing disciples for Jesus Christ than accumulating members for Wooddale Church. We welcome the opportunity to bless Christians who leave Wooddale Church to make disciples in other churches.

Kingdom-Building

The Kingdom of Jesus Christ is far greater than any local church or denomination. It includes loyal followers of Jesus all over the world. We are serious about building the kingdom. We want to give away to other churches many of the blessings God has given to us. This is done by starting new churches, encouraging hurting churches, sharing what we have learned, learning from others, sending missionaries, and much more. We rejoice when churches and Christians outside Wooddale Church prosper and succeed—and we are thrilled when God allows us to have a small part in the great good He is doing for them.

Future-Looking

Vision at Wooddale Church is in the future tense because we are future-looking. We know that faith really pleases God and faith is always forward. Our faith for the future is generated by trust in Jesus Christ. The vision that is God-centered, Bible-based, outreach-oriented, disciple-making, kingdom-building, and future-looking will supernaturally produce a healthy, growing, faithful church. Wooddale Church is like a nuclear generator powered by God, constantly releasing energy to give power and light in many directions.

Sharing the values is more than voicing the values. Every Wooddaler should be able to say them, but that's not enough. As every Wooddaler commits to our values we will pray, work, give, and do whatever needs to be done in order to turn the values we believe into the experiences we share.

We call people to Jesus Christ and the values rather than enrolling members, recruiting teachers, or raising money. Those who share the values will want to join. Those who want to make more disciples will be glad to serve. And, money will follow the values. Frankly, most of us would rather join a movement than a membership list, work for a cause rather than sign up for a job, and give to a vision rather than a budget.

Appendix C

The Personal Core Values Audit

Rate each of the following values from 1 to 5 (1 being not very important and 5 being very important).

____ 1. Godly leadership
____ 2. Individual dignity
____ 3. Multiethnic ministry
____ 4. Well-mobilized laity
____ 5. Unity
____ 6. Bible-centered exposition
____ 7. Teamwork
____ 8. The poor and disenfranchised
____ 9. Ministry's reputation
____ 10. Creativity and innovation
____ 11. Effectiveness
____ 12. World missions
____ 13. Home missions
____ 14. Dependence on God
____ 15. Importance of people
____ 16. Encouragement
____ 17. Attractive facility
____ 18. Financial responsibility
____ 19. Racial harmony/diversity
____ 20. Friendliness
____ 21. Numerical growth
____ 22. Cultural relevance
____ 23. Prayer
____ 24. Character and integrity

___25. Sustained excellence
___26. Warm fellowship
___27. Authentic community
___28. Relationships
___29. Evangelism
___30. Politics
___31. Strong families
___32. Grace orientation
___33. Equality
___34. Inspiring worship
___35. Christian self-image
___36. Efficiency
___37. Social justice
___38. Acceptance
___39. Committed Christians
___40. Stewardship
___41. Biblical counseling
___42. Civil rights
___43. Quality Christian education (all ages)
___44. Baptism and the Lord's Supper
___45. Acceptance
___46. Others:

_____
_____
_____
_____
_____
_____

Appendix D
The Corporate Core Values Audit

The following audit will help you to discover an organization's values. Directions: Observe the ministry in action and ask yourself these questions. Also, ask various people in the organization (leaders, staff, and attendees) these questions.

1. Ask for a ministry budget or financial statement. Do people give their money to this ministry? How does the ministry use its finances? What does it spend its money on?
2. Do people give of their time to the ministry? How do you know? Does the organization have a difficult time recruiting volunteers? Where are volunteers used?
3. Do talented and gifted people volunteer to serve in this ministry? If yes, why? If no, why not?
4. Are the facilities well kept? (Any peeling paint, worn carpets, water stains, and so on?) Is the equipment relatively new and in good working order? Are the grounds well maintained? Do any written materials look professional and well done?
5. Are the people excited about the ministry? Are any services exciting and upbeat? Why or why not?
6. What do people inside and outside the ministry say about it? Does it have a good or bad reputation?
7. How many people are joining the organization? Why? How many are leaving it? Why?
8. What do people like most about this ministry? What do they like least?
9. If you could change something about this organization, what would it be?
10. Are there any signs that problems exist among the staff? If yes, what?

Appendix E
The Mission Development Process

Step 1: Determine what you're supposed to be doing according to the Scriptures.
1. Are you involved in a church or parachurch ministry?
2. Whom are you attempting to serve?
3. How will you minister to people?

Step 2: Articulate your mission in a written statement.
1. What words communicate best with your people?
2. Do your people understand what you've written?
3. Does your mission format convey your mission statement well?

The mission of _____ is to
_____.

Our mission is to _____
_____.

_____ seeks to
_____.

4. Some helpful infinitives.

to assist	to develop	to establish	to produce
to create	to empower	to help	to promote
to craft	to energize	to lead	to provide
to convert	to equip	to prepare	to share

Step 3: Strike a balance between brevity and clarity.
    1. Is your mission statement broad enough?
    2. Is your mission statement clear?

Step 4: Keep it brief and simple.
    1. Have you committed information overload?
    2. Does your statement pass the T-shirt test?
    3. Can you express your mission in one sentence?
    4. Is your mission easily remembered?

Appendix F
The Vision Audit

Directions: Read each statement and circle the lette that best represents your preference in a ministry or work-related environment.

1. I tend to
    (a) dislike new problems
    (b) like new problems
2. I work best with
    (a) facts
    (b) ideas
3. I like to think about
    (a) what is
    (b) what could be
4. I like
    (a) established ways to do things
    (b) new ways to do things
5. I enjoy skills that
    (a) I have already learned and used
    (b) are newly learned but unused
6. In my work I tend to
    (a) take time to be precise
    (b) dislike taking time to be precise
7. I would describe my work style as
    (a) steady with realistic expectations
    (b) periodic with bursts of enthusiasm

8. I have found that I am
   (a) patient with routine details
   (b) impatient with routine details
9. I am more likely to trust my
   (a) experiences
   (b) inspirations
10. I am convinced that
    (a) seeing is believing
    (b) believing is seeing

Interpretation: All of the (a) responses are characteristic of nonvisionaries. All of the (b) responses are characteristic of visionaries. If you circled more *a*s than *b*s then you are a practical realist. If more *b*s than *a*s, then you are a visionary.

Appendix G
Sample Church Strategy

Mission (The Overall Goal)

The mission of the church asks: What are we supposed to be doing? The answer is the Great Commission: "To make disciples" or "to make fully devoted disciples" (Matt. 28:19–20; Mark 16:15; Luke 24:47; Acts 1:8). This is a disciple-driven mission! Therefore, the mission of this church is to turn unchurched people into fully functioning disciples of Christ.

The strategic goals (to realize the mission):

#1 To lead people to Christ and active involvement in our church (to interest in *becoming* a disciple).

#2 To help people grow to spiritual maturity (to become a *growing* disciple).

#3 To equip and involve a person in ministry both inside and outside the body of believers (to become a *serving* disciple).

#4 To enlist disciples for leadership locally and in the world (to become a disciple maker).

The Traits of a Disciple

What does a fully functioning disciple look like? How would you know one if you saw him or her? The following are some biblical, measurable, behavioral traits or characteristics of an authentic disciple.

Trait #1: A basic, growing knowledge of the Bible applied to his or her life (John 8:31–32).

We will help you to understand how the Bible is organized into the Old and New Testament and the general contents of each. You will know where to go for wisdom (Proverbs, James), worship (Psalms), and so forth. You will also gain a knowledge of basic Bible study skills. We will coach you to regularly ask the question: So what? What difference will this biblical truth make in my life, marriage, work, and so forth today, tomorrow, next year?

Trait #2: A regular devotional time (prayer, worship, and so forth) with God and the family (John 15:7–8).

We will coach and encourage you to spend regular devotional time individually and with your family. We will instruct you in the various ways to accomplish this, and you will see it modeled in the lives and families of others.

Trait #3: A daily recommitment (putting the Savior first) of one's life to Christ (Luke 9:23–25; 14:25–35).

We will encourage and exhort you to make a total commitment of your life to Christ as one of your most important life decisions. In addition, we will supply encouragement and accountability so that you might follow this up with a weekly, or better, a daily recommitment of yourself and all that you own to Him (Rom. 6–8; 12:1–2).

Trait #4: Regular attendance at church and membership in a small group (Heb. 10:25; John 13:34–35; 15:7–17; Acts 2:46; 5:42; 8:3; 20:20).

We have designed our large-group meetings to address the relevant issues of our daily lives from the Scriptures as we worship God together. We are not a church with small groups but a church of small groups. Therefore, we also want you to become a vital part of one of our vibrant small groups where much of our discipleship takes place.

Trait #5: Understands his or her divine design and is involved in a ministry (1 Tim. 4:14; 2 Tim. 1:6; Eph. 4:11–13).

God has wonderfully designed all of us in a unique way to serve Him. He has called and gifted us to be his servants whether inside or outside the four walls of the church. It is our goal to help you discover who you are, like who you are, and be who you are as you serve the Savior.

Trait #6: Building relationships and sharing the faith ("a fisher of men") with lost people at home and abroad (Matt. 9:36–38).

Because lost people matter to God, they matter to us (Luke 15; 19:1–10). We desire to do whatever it takes to help you reach the toughest mission field of your life—your neighbors, family, and workmates.

Trait #7: A generous, joyful giver (2 Corinthians 8).

All that we possess is a gracious gift from God that ultimately belongs to Him. Therefore, we will provide you with instruction on biblical giving and encourage you to invest in God's work through this ministry.

(Note: These traits are found below in parenthesis next to the objective that accomplishes them.)

Strategy

The following strategy is how we move people from prebirth to maturity. It consists of four levels. The word *level* implies level of commitment. The range is from level 1 (the least amount of commitment) up to level 4 (the maximum amount of commitment).

Level 1: Interesting People in Christ

Goal

To lead people to Christ and active involvement in the church (to interest in *becoming* a disciple) (Luke 15:1–10; 19:1–10; Col. 4:2–6; 2 Tim. 4:4; 1 Cor. 14:22–25). To call unchurched lost and saved people (young people as well as adults) out of the stands (world) and onto the playing field (serious, authentic Christianity).

Actions

1. A seeker-friendly large-group meeting to interest lost and saved young people and adults in becoming disciples. This is a "front door" event.
   a. Sermon—mostly topical that teaches biblical truth and shows its relevancy to everyday life.
   b. Drama—short, relevant accounts that set up or introduce the sermon topic and/or make application to life.
   c. Worship—contemporary, celebratory music led by a praise band.
   d. Prayer—a time of public prayer for the world, nation, and community.

e. Evangelism—a regular presentation of the Gospel through sermons, drama, and other events.

2. A small group to lead people to Christ and/or orient them to the church (its expectations, beliefs, programs, and so forth). It loves and cares for them as well. These groups are in the early stages of initiating the disciple-making process. They are explaining what the church is all about and inviting those in the group to move on with Christ. Those who stick go on with this group to phase 2. (**Trait #4**).

   a. Basic small groups for people. These are communities that minister to all ages from children's groups to older adult groups. (The small-group approach will replace the traditional Sunday school for our children and young people.) The ordinances (Lord's Supper and baptism) will take place in this context.

   b. Special small groups for special people: twelve step groups, addiction groups, abuse groups, women's and men's groups, premarriage groups, divorce recovery groups, and so forth.

3. Other events (to minister to people and hold them in the church). Vacation Bible school, aerobics, choir, Pioneer Boys and Girls clubs, Awana, sports events, and others.

Time

How long should a person be at level 1? Six months? One to two years? (Pastor Lee Strobel of Willow Creek Community Church needed two years).

(Note: Both the large-group and the small-group leaders constantly invite these people to become fully functioning disciples, that is, to move to level 2 and in time the other levels.)

Level 2: Growing in Christ

Goal

To help people grow to spiritual maturity (to become a *growing* disciple) (Col. 1:28; Eph. 4:12–13; 1 Tim. 4:7–8; Heb. 6:1–3).

Action

Discipleship Small Groups (fully functioning communities)

Lay pastor-leaders will be responsible to equip the people in their small groups directly or through a seminar given by a specialist in our church in each of the following key areas that are essential to becoming a disciple:

1. Scripture—gain a knowledge of the Bible, theology, and how to study the Bible on one's own (**Trait #1**).

2. Prayer—to learn about and practice private and public prayer (**Trait #2**).
3. Worship—to learn how to worship and to practice private and public worship (**Trait #2**).
4. Evangelism—to discover one's evangelism style and begin to share the Gospel with the lost in his or her relational group, community, and the world (missions) (**Trait #6**).
5. Giving—to learn about and practice biblical giving (**Trait #7**).
6. Commitment—to learn the importance of and commit to attending the meetings of the church. More important to commit one's life to the Lord daily (**Traits #3 & #4**).

Time
One to two years?

Level 3: Ministering in Christ

Goal

To equip people for and involve them in ministry (to become a *serving* disciple) (Eph. 4:11–12; 1 Cor. 12:12–31; Rom. 12:1–8; 1 Tim. 4:14). This lay mobilization primarily involves helping people to discover their divine design, direction, and ministry placement so that they can become Christ's servants (servanthood). This phase provides the committed workers whose ministry may take place within the four walls of the church or outside in the local community—-inner-city mission, church planting, and so on.

Action
1. The person will continue in his/her discipleship small group while at this level and after they have completed it. Disciples thrive on community and will always need one another (see all the "one another" passages in the New Testament). It's practically impossible to grow without a group.
2. A staff or lay minister of involvement will visit the group for several weeks and take them through the lay mobilization process (**Trait #5**).
3. A staff or lay minister of involvement will match the disciples with the church's ministries for which they are best suited according to their design. If there is no existing match, they may start a new ministry. However, we will start no ministries without a leader. Those in the current ministry are responsible to train the disciple recruit. The disciple as Christ's servant will continue to minister inside or outside the church for the duration of his or her time at the church and hopefully the rest of his or her life.

Time

One to three months?

Level 4: Leading in Christ

Goal

To enlist disciples as lay and professional leaders of ministries at home and abroad (to become disciple makers) (1 Tim. 3:1–13; Titus 1:1–9; Acts 6:1–7; 2 Tim. 2:2). This is the all-important servant leadership and followership development phase. It involves taking others around the base paths. It is where you equip and develop the gifted men and women who will become vital lay workers, small-group leaders, deacons, elders, church staff, church planters, and missionaries of the church (**Trait #6**). Therefore, you as a pastor and staff will pour much of your time into this stage and these critical people. Note that this is a process and no one becomes a leader or server overnight (the "warm body" approach)! Interns from seminaries, Bible colleges, and Christian schools will do their internships at this level.

Note: The desire is that everyone move to and through this level. It is a must for leaders and leadership development. The staff and small group leaders in particular look for gifted leaders (including mature teenagers) and individually invite and encourage them to consider moving on to level 4. Lay people in key positions other than leadership should also move to this level because their ministry results in directly or indirectly making disciples.

Action

1. The prospective leader must meet certain requirements for leadership (1 Timothy 3; Titus 2; Acts 6), depending on his or her anticipated ministry (small group, staff, church planter, and other positions).
2. The prospective leader (including interns) will begin as an apprentice leader who assists a small group leader. No one simply walks in and becomes a leader overnight.
3. The apprentice leader will develop leadership skills (handwork) working with or in the small group three weeks a month (on-the-job training) and will gain leadership knowledge (headwork) attending a CKS meeting (character, knowledge, skills training session) once a month (excluding summers).
4. Leaders who foresee full-time ministry will be mentored one-on-one by someone on the pastoral staff, depending on their future ministry goals.

5. Those not in leadership positions will receive advanced training in their ministry-skills areas.

Time

Long term commitment. (Interns—six months to one year.)

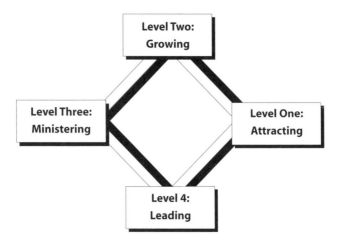

Comments

The following comments provide some explanation that will help you to further understand this strategy and the rationale behind the decisions that affected it.

1. Every goal must have a corresponding action that implements it. A goal without an action is like a carpenter without a hammer or a surgeon without a scalpel.
2. It has been my experience (and that of others) that becoming a growing disciple (level 2) precedes becoming a serving or ministering disciple (level 3). The maturity that is gained in level 2 produces fruit in the form of ministry or service in level 3. This is the rationale behind having four levels.
3. The staff pastors in this system are more trainers (coaches) than doers (ministers). For example, the heavy teaching will not take place at the level 1 seeker friendly large-group meeting on Saturday or Sunday that are led by the staff. It will take place under the ministry of lay leaders in the small-group meetings at level 2 and other meetings such as seminars. This means that the staff pastors will train the lay pastors in how to teach the deeper truths of Scripture (Eph. 4:11; 2 Tim. 2:2).
4. In a church where there are two or more staff pastors, the preaching

in the seeker-friendly large-group meeting will be shared by the pastors. The point person will preach perhaps 60 percent of the sermons and the support staff the other 40 percent. Consequently, should the point person leave, the church survives the loss.

5. You will need to answer the question: What purpose do the large-group and the small-group meetings serve? Quite frankly, it is naive to believe that the large-group meeting (sermon) is sufficient in itself to disciple anyone! I know of no one who has seriously studied the disciple-making process who believes that it is. The key method in disciple making is the small group along with solid biblical preaching and teaching. That is how the Savior and others in the New Testament (Paul, Barnabas, and others) did it.

6. The measure of success in this system is not how well you know the Bible and theology nor your ability to sight-read the Old and New Testaments from the original languages, and so on. While these are important, the biblical measure of your success is your disciples (Col. 1:28–29; 2 Cor. 3:1–6; Eph. 5:25–27). Where are your disciples? (If disciple-making is what the church and ministry are all about, then perhaps a requirement for graduation from seminaries should not be good grades but mature disciples.)

7. The fully functioning small-group approach will replace any traditional Sunday school lecture-them-to-discipleship approach for all ages. While we may have a nontraditional Sunday school program, the children, for example, will be in their own age group small group with a lay pastor-leader who may be an adult or possibly a mature level 3 or 4 teen leader.

8. Our programs are set up to minister to churched and unchurched, lost and saved whether children, young people, or adults, and those who are emotionally healthy as well as those who struggle with various addictions.

9. The implementation of the various parts of this strategy is dependent on having the right people to lead them. Rather than use anyone, we will wait until we have the right person for the ministry before implementing that ministry. We will determine this based on our Divine Design Program as led by a lay or staff ministry consultant who will assist our people in discovering their ministry designs and directions and then help place them.

10. The senior or point pastor is responsible for coordinating all four levels. He will recruit, develop, and work with a gifted, qualified lay person or professional staff person to lead at each level. Preferably this person would be a lay person (especially in smaller churches and church planting, however, the problem here is turnover in our highly mobile culture). The leaders at each level are the

following. Level 1: a pastor or director of programming or worship. Level 2: a pastor or director of small groups or ministries or Christian education. Level 3: a pastor or director of involvement or administration. Level 4: a pastor or director of leadership development. These leaders, in turn, will recruit and develop a team to minister at each level. They will be evaluated on how well they recruit their teams and produce results in each of their areas.

11. It is critical that everyone on the leadership team embrace the mission and the general strategy. That includes board members, professional and lay staff. Consequently, any discussions and disagreements will be over the details not the general direction.

12. As God provides various people with gifts, talents, and knowledge of certain special areas, they will offer to help train our people in a class or seminar format. This would include such areas as Bible study methods, books of the Bible, areas of theology, prayer, finances, evangelism, apologetics, and so on. The various small groups may pull together for a seminar or the instructor may visit the small group.

Index